Salvation in the Orthodox Understanding

Salvation in the Orthodox Understanding

H.H. POPE SHENOUDA III

Translated by
St. Mary and St. Moses Abbey

Salvation in the Orthodox Understanding
By H.H. Pope Shenouda III

Translated from Arabic by St. Mary & St. Moses Abbey.

Designed & Published by:
St. Mary & St. Moses Abbey Press
101 S Vista Dr., Sandia, TX 78383
stmabbeypress.com

Cover icon of Christ was written by the iconographer Gergis Samir.

Contents

✠

Forward

This study, written by H.G. Abba Shenouda,[1] Bishop for Religious Institutes and Church Education, is clear, precise, and holistic, which is on one of the most important subjects that has occupied the mind of the believers throughout the ages, because it is connected to the issue of salvation, the purpose of the faith, and the crown of the Christian hope, and so on.

In this study, you see the upright Orthodox teaching, proven through sound logic and proper use of the Holy Scriptures, revealing the erroneous understanding.

I testify that this valuable book is capable of treating the subject of salvation satisfactorily for the first time, sufficient to give a bright, true picture of the teaching of our Orthodox Church regarding the issue of salvation.

Greghorius

By the grace of God, General Bishop for High Theological Studies, Coptic Culture, and Scientific Research

---

1   The late H.H. Pope Shenouda III before his papacy.

Introduction

The Danger of Using a Single Verse

On the subject of salvation, my brethren, as on any other subject, be very careful about the danger of using a single verse from the Holy Scriptures. The Holy Scriptures are not merely a verse or verses, but rather are a particular spirit permeating through the entire Book.

The foolish person places before themselves a single verse, or parts of a verse, isolating it from its context, circumstances, and the whole general meaning. As for the wise researcher, who is aiming for the truth, they collect all the texts pertaining to the subject matter of their research, and [then] see what they indicate.

On the subject of salvation, we see examples of the danger of using a single verse.

"Believe on the Lord Jesus Christ, and you will be saved, you and your household."[2]

Some take this verse as proof of salvation by faith only, because in this verse St. Paul the Apostle says to the keeper of the prison of Philippi, "Believe… and you will be saved." Those who use this verse forget several things: to whom was it said? What is the rest of the verse? What happened after it? And what are the other verses connected to the subject?

1. This verse was said to a Gentile, an unbeliever. No matter how many good works he does, they will not benefit him at all

---

2   Acts 16:31.

without believing in Christ. Therefore, it was necessary that he be directed to the first step, without which he cannot receive salvation. If he takes this step, then he can be directed to the subsequent steps. It was not appropriate for the two apostles to speak to this jailor about the importance of good works, because these cannot benefit him while he is an unbeliever. The proper state is that they advance gradually with him, step by step, until he reaches [salvation].

2. The first step is sometimes used in the Holy Scriptures to indicate the entire work beginning with that step. An example of this is the saying of Simeon the elder when he took up the Child Jesus in his arms: "Lord, now You are letting Your servant depart in peace, according to Your word; for my eyes have seen Your salvation,"[3] although Simeon the elder did not see the salvation of the Lord, which was not accomplished except by the blood of Christ on the cross, when the Lord paid the price of sin by His death for us. Simeon, however, saw only the incarnation of the Lord and His birth. Since the incarnation of the Lord is the first executed step which leads to salvation, Simeon the elder, therefore, confidently said, "For my eyes have seen Your salvation."

In nearly the same manner, Paul and Silas spoke with the jailor of Philippi, not that his faith only was that which would save him and his household, but rather that this was the first step leading to all that.

And perhaps in this manner also, when Zacchaeus promised to restore fourfold what he had robbed from people, the Lord said to him, "Today salvation has come to this house."[4] That is to say, Zacchaeus' repentance was the first step that would lead to the salvation of the house.

3. The greatest proof that what is meant by this salvation is the first step leading to it, is the saying of the apostle to this jailer, "You will be saved, you and your household." For how can his household be saved through his faith only? Does the faith of a person save another?

---

3   Luke 2:29–30.
4   Luke 19:9.

The sound understanding[5] is that the faith of this person is only the first step, which will lead him to salvation when he is baptized in the name of Jesus Christ, and so he will be saved and his household.

4. Therefore, we see that this verse has an ending. For the Scripture says that Paul and Silas "spoke the word of the Lord to him and to all who were in his house.... And immediately he and all his family were baptized."[6]

5. If we take this verse, "Believe on the Lord Jesus Christ, and you will be saved, you and your household," we need to put beside it other verses to fully understand this subject. I will mention a simple example that has its powerful indications:

A young man approached the Lord Christ to ask Him, "What good thing shall I do that I may have eternal life?"[7] The Lord Christ did not say to him, "Believe and you will be saved," but He said to him, "If you want to enter into life, keep the commandments."[8]

Are we so bold as to say that the mere keeping of the commandments is sufficient for salvation—without faith, without Baptism, and without the Mysteries? No, we should not wrong ourselves, nor the people, nor the faith itself, by using a single verse.

In this example also, we find that when the young man said about the commandments, "All these things I have kept from my youth. What do I still lack?"[9] Then our Lord Jesus said to him, "If you want to be perfect, go, sell what you have and give to the poor, and you will have treasure in heaven; and come, follow Me."[10] Here also the Lord Christ did not speak to him about faith—nor about grace. So, do we use this example to diminish the value of faith, for it was not mentioned in the Lord's speech on receiving eternal life? No, God forbid that we do this and use a single verse, for there are suitable words for every situation[11]. And in this example, the Lord

---

5   Literally: state.
6   Acts 16:32–33.
7   Matthew 19:16.
8   Matthew 19:17.
9   Matthew 19:20.
10 Matthew 19:21.
11 Literally: domain, field.

spoke to the rich young man with what suits his state, and with what treats his original, inner sicknesses.

Let us treat another verse of those verses that are used by the Protestants and by those walking in their course.

"Therefore, having been justified by faith, we have peace with God"[12]

A man, of those interested in the single verse, comes and says to you, "Here is a clear verse in front of you, saying that justification is by faith; therefore, there is no point in arguing or [even] opening your mouth! Do you reject this verse or go against the word of God?"

No, my brother, we neither reject the verse, nor do we go against the word of God; rather, we put other verses beside this verse, from the same epistle of St. Paul the Apostle to the Romans, and [then] we see what can be understood from that verse. The Apostle says, "For not the hearers of the law are just in the sight of God, but the doers of the law will be justified."[13]

The word here is about the justification of the doers of the law. So do we allow ourselves to fall into error and use a single verse, saying that works alone are those which save, relying on the saying of the apostle: "But the doers of the law will be justified"? No; rather, we put both verses together (Romans 2:13 and 5:1) and come out with the right teaching that is in agreement with the word of God. That is to say, the role of faith in justification does not deny the importance of works; neither does the requirement of works for justification deny the value of faith.

Besides this verse that says "having been justified by faith," we put another verse: "You see then that a man is justified by works, and not by faith only. Likewise, was not Rahab the harlot also justified by works when she received the messengers and sent them out another way?"[14] Let us take another verse.

---

12   Romans 5:1.
13   Romans 2:13.
14   James 2:24–25.

"But to him who does not work but believes on Him who justifies the ungodly, his faith is accounted for righteousness."[15]

Does this verse mean that God justifies the ungodly if they persist in their ungodliness, without the work of repentance? Absolutely not! Therefore, in order to understand this verse, let us put before it other verses that clarify it. Let us begin with a verse from the same epistle to the Romans, in which the apostle says, "For the wrath of God is revealed from heaven against all ungodliness and unrighteousness of men."[16]

Let us add another verse to this from the second epistle of St. Peter the Apostle, "Turning the cities of Sodom and Gomorrah into ashes, condemned them to destruction, making them an example to those who afterward would live ungodly."[17] And so the apostle revealed to us that the ungodly take part in the fate of Sodom and Gomorrah.

Our teacher Jude also explains this to us, saying, "Now Enoch, the seventh from Adam, prophesied about these men also, saying, 'Behold, the Lord comes with ten thousands of His saints, to execute judgment on all, to convict all who are ungodly among them of all their ungodly deeds which they have committed in an ungodly way.'"[18]

Therefore, from the verse that St. Paul the Apostle said, it is not possible to understand that it is sufficient for the ungodly to only believe, so that they are saved, while remaining in their ungodliness. For St. Paul himself warned us very explicitly,[19] saying, "Do not be deceived. Neither fornicators, nor idolaters, nor adulterers, nor homosexuals, nor sodomites, ... will inherit the kingdom of God."[20]

---

15 Romans 4:5.
16 Romans 1:18.
17 2 Peter 2:6.
18 Jude 1:14–15.
19 Literally: with utter frankness.
20 1 Corinthians 6:9–10.

As for the phrase "does not work," perhaps what is meant by it here is the ritualistic works of the law, such as the circumcision in particular, as it is made apparent from the rest of the passage (Romans 5:6–12). My beloved, it is absolutely incorrect that we walk in the way of "the single verse," for this way is erroneous, dangerous, and unorthodox.

If one day someone brings a verse to you, no matter how explicit and clear it may be, say to the person, "A single verse does me no good; let us place before us all the texts linked to this subject, and then we will talk." Beware of being deceived by "the single verse": for it may have a particular context, and it may have a remainder, and this remainder is that which would clarify its meaning. I will give you some examples of this.

Verses That are Clarified by Their Remainder

St. Paul the Apostle says in his epistle to the Ephesians, "For by grace you have been saved through faith, and that not of yourselves; it is the gift of God, not of works, lest anyone should boast."[21] This verse may seem explicit; wait a little, however, and read the verse right after it. He says, "For we are His workmanship, created in Christ Jesus for good works, which God prepared beforehand that we should walk in them."[22] It is not befitting, therefore, that we snatch a verse and run with it, saying lightly that the matter is over.

Let us take another example. St. Paul the Apostle says, "And if by grace, then it is no longer of works; otherwise grace is no longer grace."[23] How beautiful it is that we slow down a little and follow what the apostle is saying in the same chapter. For he continues, saying, "Do not be haughty, but fear. For if God did not spare the natural branches, He may not spare you either. Therefore, consider the goodness and severity of God: on those who fell, severity; but toward you, goodness, if you continue in His goodness. Otherwise,

---

21 Ephesians 2:8–9.
22 Ephesians 2:10.
23 Romans 11:6.

you also will be cut off."[24] What is the meaning of this? It means that you received salvation by the blood of Christ, but you must continue in it. Otherwise, you will lose it if you do not do works befitting repentance. For the branch that is cut off from the tree is lost and dies.

Here is another example. St. Paul the Apostle says, "Where is boasting then? It is excluded. By what law? Of works? No, but by the law of faith. Therefore, we conclude that a man is justified by faith apart from the deeds of the law."[25] If we read a verse like this one, we should not be hasty, but we should continue reading to see what the apostle says after it. He continues after this verse directly, saying, "Do we then make void the law through faith? Certainly not! On the contrary, we establish the law."[26]

And here is yet another example. St. Paul the Apostle says, "But when the kindness and the love of God our Savior toward man appeared, not by works of righteousness which we have done, but according to His mercy He saved us, through the washing of regeneration and renewing of the Holy Spirit."[27] Note that this verse in particular speaks about salvation through Baptism and the work of the Holy Spirit. But concerning works, if we finish what the apostle is saying, we find that he continues directly, saying, "This is a faithful saying, and these things I want you to affirm constantly, that those who have believed in God should be careful to maintain good works. These things are good and profitable to men."[28]

Beloved brethren, I am not discussing in this introduction the subject of faith and works, for its time in this book has not yet come. Rather, I would only like to direct the attention to this rule alone: that is, the danger of using a single verse. And we do not at all permit ourselves to use this dangerous, harmful way.

---

24 Romans 11:20–22. Also see Romans 11:10–20.
25 Romans 3:27–28.
26 Romans 3:31.
27 Titus 3:4–5. See also Titus 3:6.
28 Titus 3:8.

We do not Exploit "the Single Verse" to Our Advantage

For example, if we find St. John the Apostle say, "If you know that He is righteous, you know that everyone who practices righteousness is born of Him,"[29] we must not say that the new birth depends on works alone; rather, with this verse, we mention faith, Baptism, and the Mysteries, which this verse did not include at all with respect to the utterance [i.e., the exact wording of the verse].

Likewise also if we read the saying of St. John the Apostle, "We know that we have passed from death to life, because we love the brethren,"[30] we must not take this verse as a proof that love alone is sufficient to save a person and to make them pass from death to life.

Also in the same manner, we must not exploit the verse that says, "God is love, and he who abides in love abides in God, and God in him."[31]

And we must not likewise exploit any verse of the verses speaking about works and their importance, for example, the word of the Lord Christ to the rich young man: "If you want to enter into life, keep the commandments."[32] Is the mere keeping of the commandments alone sufficient, without faith and without Baptism? No, without a doubt. The verse, however, is understood with another meaning that is in agreement with the circumstances surrounding it.

And so, beloved, we must continually remember, in our recognition of the sound faith, the beautiful verse that says, "Not of the letter but of the Spirit; for the letter kills, but the Spirit gives life."[33] Therefore, let us then search for the understanding of salvation, being led by the Spirit of the Book, not its letter, trying to collect on one level the various texts that deal with the subject. Let us approach our subject from all its aspects, and not from one angle only, nor in a particular context only.

---

29   1 John 2:29.
30   1 John 3:14.
31   1 John 4:16.
32   Matthew 19:17.
33   2 Corinthians 3:6.

My advice to you is that you stay away from the foreign books that distance you from sound faith. My advice also is that you research a subject in profound humility, because, in theological matters, self-esteem has led many to fall into heresy.

After this concise introduction, we will speak about salvation in the Orthodox understanding and its means.

CHAPTER ONE

No Salvation Except by the Blood of Christ Alone

Neither Faith nor Works Without This Blood

Faith is the faith in the blood of Christ, and works are the works founded on the merits we receive through the blood of Christ, as St. Paul the Apostle says, "Without shedding of blood there is no remission."[34] What is then the status of the blood of Christ in the issue of salvation? What is the status of faith? And what is the status of works?

Works Without the Blood of Christ

There is no salvation except by the blood of Christ. All the works, no matter how sublime they are, no matter how elevated, no matter how perfect—they cannot save a person without the blood of Christ. For this reason, all the righteous, who pleased the Lord with their works in the Old Testament, also waited in Hades until the Lord Christ took them out of it after His crucifixion.

Good works alone cannot save a person without faith in the blood of Christ. Otherwise, all the Pagans who had good works would be saved through their works! God forbid.

As a general rule, which I would like to say, all the verses mentioned in the Holy Scriptures that attack works are about works alone, without the blood of Christ, or are about the works of

---

34   Hebrews 9:22.

the law belonging to the Old Testament.

For without the blood of Christ, works are of no benefit at all. Therefore, when the apostle says, "Not by works of righteousness which we have done,"[35] or when he says, "Not of works, lest anyone should boast,"[36] he rather means the works alone, without the blood of Christ. And so, if a person is found doing good works, while he is an unbeliever, then this righteousness of the law does not benefit him at all, and his good works alone do not save him, without faith. To such an unbelieving person, you say, "All your works are not sufficient. Believe on the Lord Jesus, and you will be saved."

There is a fundamental, essential difference between words said to a believer and words said to an unbeliever. In your speech with the unbeliever, you must destroy all the works. All of them, without the blood of Christ, benefit nothing. To such a person, you say, "Your works do not save you; that which saves you is the blood of Christ." The blood of Christ is the starting point in the subject of salvation. After the person believes, however, you must speak to him about the good works befitting his faith, because "faith without works is dead."[37]

Why is There no Salvation Except by the Blood of Christ?

1. Sin is a disobedience against God, a trespass against His rights, and a lack of love for Him. God is infinite; therefore, sin is infinite, because it is directed against the infinite God. And no matter how much a person works, their works are finite; therefore, sin is not forgiven except by an infinite propitiation. And no one is infinite except God; therefore, there was no solution for the forgiveness of sin except that God Himself becomes incarnate and dies. His death would be an infinite propitiation that fulfills the infinite justice of God, in retribution for the infinite sin that is directed against the infinite God.

---

35   Titus 3:5.
36   Ephesians 2:9.
37   James 2:20.

2. This word applies to Adam's sin as well as to any person's sin, because sin is the same, and God's justice is the same, and the punishment for sin, that is death, is the same, in the Old Testament and the New Testament. And it is known that "they have all turned aside… there is none who does good, no, not one,"[38] and, "For all have sinned and fall short of the glory of God."[39] And so the sentence of death befell all, and every mouth was stopped, and all the world became guilty before God.[40] And there was no means for salvation, except that the grace of God visits us, and it indeed visited us and saved us by the blood of Christ, by which only is salvation.

3. For this reason our teacher Paul the Apostle said, "Being justified freely by His grace through the redemption that is in Christ Jesus, whom God set forth as a propitiation by His blood, through faith, to demonstrate His righteousness, because in His forbearance God had passed over the sins that were previously committed," [41] and he said, "Who has saved us and called us with a holy calling, not according to our works, but according to His own purpose and grace which was given to us,"[42] and he also said, "Not by works of righteousness which we have done, but according to His mercy He saved us, through the washing of regeneration and renewing of the Holy Spirit,"[43] and he likewise said, "For by grace you have been saved through faith, and that not of yourselves; it is the gift of God, not of works, lest anyone should boast,"[44] and he said, "And if by grace, then it is no longer of works; otherwise grace is no longer grace."[45]

We have quoted these verses, which the Protestants use, and have not concealed them, because we do not deny the grace of God for us; neither do we deny the free salvation of God, which He gave to us, nor do we deny that all of us "were dead in trespasses and

---

38   Romans 3:12.

39   Romans 3:23.

40   See Romans 3:19.

41   Romans 3:24–25.

42   2 Timothy 1:9.

43   Titus 3:5.

44   Ephesians 2:8.

45   Romans 11:6.

sins,"[46] and if it had not been for His holy blood, all of us would have perished. Rather, we put these verses in their true context and confess that we were saved by the blood of Christ.

4. We, however, say that the blood of Christ is one thing, and being worthy of the blood of Christ is another. The blood of Christ is sufficient for the forgiveness of the sins of the whole world; so, has the whole world obtained forgiveness? "For God so loved the world that He gave His only begotten Son,"[47] so, was the whole world saved by this giving, or only "whoever believes in Him"[48] was saved?

Then the blood of Christ is present, ready to save, sufficient for salvation. Salvation, however, has conditions that ought to be met, so that the sinner may be worthy of this blood, by which is salvation. And so St. John the beloved also says in his first epistle concerning Christ, that "He Himself is the propitiation for our sins, and not for ours only but also for the whole world."[49] Then the propitiation of Christ is infinite, sufficient to forgive all the sins, of all people, in all generations, in the past, present, and future.

Despite the presence of the blood of Christ, there are nevertheless some people who perished, and others who are perishing, and yet others who will perish! This is because there are particular conditions for the merits we receive by the blood of Christ.

The Conditions of Salvation by the Blood of Christ

Regarding these conditions, I would like to place before you four very essential matters:

1. Faith

2. Baptism

3. The Church Mysteries that are necessary for salvation

4. Good works

---

46   Ephesians 2:1.

47   John 3:16.

48   Ibid.

49   1 John 2:2.

Faith

1. The Condition of Faith

Faith is a fundamental condition to become worthy of the blood of Christ. And so did the Lord Christ say about Himself, "… that whoever believes in Him should not perish but have everlasting life."[50] And the importance of this condition to become worthy of the blood of Christ is made manifest in the saying of the Scripture in the same chapter by the mouth of the Lord Christ Himself, "He who believes in Him is not condemned; but he who does not believe is condemned already, because he has not believed in the name of the only begotten Son of God."[51]

This condition is also made manifest in the saying of St. John the Apostle at the end of his gospel, "But these are written that you may believe that Jesus is the Christ, the Son of God, and that believing you may have life in His name."[52] There is a condition, then: that is, you would have salvation if you believed. This also did Paul the Apostle preach in Antioch, saying, "Through this Man is preached to you the forgiveness of sins; and by Him everyone who believes is justified."[53]

Our Lord Jesus Christ clarified that, without this condition of faith, there cannot be salvation, by saying to the Jews, "If you do not believe that I am He, you will die in your sins."[54] How alarming this statement is: "You will die in your sins." The blood of Christ is present and is able to save, but it cannot save you without you.

You must present the condition of faith, so that you may be saved by the blood of Christ. It is the first condition, but it is not the only one. It is the step that qualifies you for Baptism. The condition of faith was mentioned in the words of Paul and Silas to the keeper of the prison: "Believe on the Lord Jesus Christ, and you

---

50   John 3:16.
51   John 3:18.
52   John 20:31.
53   Acts 13:38–39.
54   John 8:24.

will be saved, you and your household."[55]

2. What is Faith?

The word "faith" is a very broad word, in which many matters are incorporated. St. Paul the Apostle said, "Having been justified by faith,"[56] so what does he mean by this faith, by which we have been justified? Therefore, St. Paul the Apostle puts in front of us an exceedingly serious question on the subject of faith. He says, "Examine yourselves as to whether you are in the faith. Test yourselves."[57] We must then test ourselves to see whether we are truly in the faith or not. What is this faith?

A Living Faith

The faith that is necessary for salvation must be a living faith. And this matter was explained to the fullest by our teacher James the Apostle, who said, "Faith without works is dead,"[58] and he repeated this sense, saying, "For as the body without the spirit is dead, so faith without works is dead also."[59] Such a dead faith, that is the faith devoid of works, cannot save anyone. And so does our teacher James the Apostle say, "What does it profit, my brethren, if someone says he has faith but does not have works? Can faith save him?"[60]

It is true that the Apostle said that we were justified by faith, but this faith has two important qualities: a living faith and a working faith. And in both of these qualities, we see the good works.

And do not think that any Protestant, no matter how intensely they deny works, can, in the issue of salvation, teach about the nonworking faith. For the apostle says, "Even the demons believe—and tremble!"[61] Therefore, do you mean by faith, brother, a faith of the kind of faith of the demons that do not have good works, but

---

55   Acts 16:31.
56   Romans 5:1.
57   2 Corinthians 13:5.
58   James 2:20.
59   James 2:26.
60   James 2:14.
61   James 2:19.

they believe and tremble from the atrocity of their wickedness and corruption?

The phrase "the living, working faith" may expand in its extent to encompass the whole spiritual life. How does it encompass the whole spiritual life? Beloved brethren, incline your ears to the saying of the Apostle.

Faith Working Through Love

St. Paul the Apostle said, "For in Christ Jesus neither circumcision nor uncircumcision avails anything, but faith working through love."[62] What does the characteristic "working through love" mean? What is this love, and how can it be?

St. Paul the Apostle explained this love, inferring it from a multitude of good works, saying, "Love suffers long and is kind; love does not envy; love does not parade itself, is not puffed up; does not behave rudely, does not seek its own, is not provoked, thinks no evil; does not rejoice in iniquity, but rejoices in the truth; bears all things, believes all things, hopes all things, endures all things."[63]

If faith were this faith working through love, then it would undoubtedly encompass all these qualities—and all of them are works. Here Christianity seems in its essence to be not just a verse, but is spirit and life.[64] Truly [it is] as the Scripture said, "The letter kills, but the Spirit gives life."[65] The letter here says to you that there is something called faith, but the Spirit explains to you the essence of the faith, and that it encompasses all the good works.

Therefore, do our opposing brethren mean faith with this vast meaning that encompasses the whole spiritual life, and do they mean faith with the great meaning, to which Paul the Apostle referred in the eleventh chapter of the epistle to the Hebrews when he spoke about the men of faith? Or do they mean mere faith that

---

62   Galatians 5:6.
63   1 Corinthians 13:4–7.
64   See John 6:63.
65   2 Corinthians 3:6.

is devoid of its aforementioned qualities? If the matter is so, let us discuss [further], so that we may see whether this faith can save them, as St. James the Apostle marveled.

3. Faith and Love

Those who say that faith alone is that which justifies a person, establishing faith as a stand-alone element, far removed from works—those [people], it is not I who stop them, but it is St. Paul the Apostle who stops them before a tremendous verse that says, "Though I have all faith, so that I could remove mountains, but have not love, I am nothing."[66] So do you want a greater faith than this?

And you, brother, no matter how high you grow in faith, what is the highest degree you will reach? Will you reach all faith that removes mountains? Believe me when I say that even if you have reached this degree also, and you have not love, you are nothing! This faith cannot save you. If Paul the Apostle, with all his faith, is nothing without love, how much more are you?

Therefore, the apostle placed love on a level greater than faith, saying, "Now abide faith, hope, love, these three; but the greatest of these is love."[67]

4. The Believers and the Elect

We said that faith must be a living faith and a faith working through love. Some, however, exaggerate sometimes in defining the word "believers" to the extent that it becomes synonymous with the word "elect." And so, such people proclaim that the believer cannot perish. And if they hear or read that a believer has perished, they say that this [person] was not a believer according to their own understanding! Undoubtedly, the elect cannot perish, but who said that the believers are the elect?

The Holy Scriptures have given us many meanings for the word "faith." For the Scripture mentioned once that "even the

---

66   1 Corinthians 13:2.

67   1 Corinthians 13:13.

demons believe—and tremble!"[68] And St. Paul the Apostle said in his definition of faith that "faith is the substance of things hoped for, the evidence of things not seen."[69]

The Scriptures explained to us that there is a kind of faith that is dead. And although it is dead, the Apostle nevertheless called it faith. And he has given us an example of faith that is devoid of works, which cannot save anyone.[70] And although it cannot save anyone, the apostle nevertheless called it faith.

The Scriptures also mentioned that "they have all turned aside; they have together become unprofitable.... and fall short of the glory of God."[71] So were "all" unbelievers, and was the earth devoid of faith? Or did God use the title "faith" even on those who sin while they are believers?

The Lord did not deprive such sinners as those of the title "believers." For the Lord said on the tongue of Jeremiah the prophet, "For My people have committed two evils: They have forsaken Me, the fountain of living waters, and hewn themselves cisterns—broken cisterns that can hold no water.... Yet My people have forgotten Me days without number."[72] With all this, He called them "His people." He also said on the tongue of Isaiah the prophet: "I have nourished and brought up children, and they have rebelled against Me."[73] Despite their rebellion, He called them "children." And this reminds us of what he said about the prodigal son, "For this my son was dead and is alive again; he was lost and is found."[74] And despite his being lost and his spiritual death, he called him "son."

In the saying of the apostle, "Though I have all faith, so that I could remove mountains, but have not love, I am nothing,"[75]

---

68   James 2:19.
69   Hebrews 11:1.
70   See James 2:14, 20.
71   Romans 3:12, 23.
72   Jeremiah 2:13, 32.
73   Isaiah 1:2.
74   Luke 15:24.
75   1 Corinthians 13:2.

[this is] another proof for attributing the state of faith to a person devoid of love, who is nothing. Even the Lord called them by the title "believers," those who were like the seed that fell on rock, and when they sprang up, they withered away. He said, "Some fell on rock; and as soon as it sprang up, it withered away because it lacked moisture.... and these have no root, who believe for a while and in time of temptation fall away."[76]

Of course, those who fall away we cannot call "the elect," although the Lord Christ—glory be to Him—gave them the title of believers, of being believers for a while. These, of course, resemble those of whom the apostle said, "Now the Spirit expressly says that in latter times some will depart from the faith, giving heed to deceiving spirits and doctrines of demons."[77] And those, of course, we cannot call "the elect," although they lived in the faith before they fell away.

Perhaps it has become very clear now that there is a great difference between the two words: all the elect are believers, but not all the believers are the elect, for some might fall away from the faith, giving heed to deceiving spirits and doctrines of demons.

Beloved, we will return to this point after a while. We leave it now for a little while to speak about the second condition for salvation and the fundamental entrance to it: that is, Baptism.

Baptism

The Importance of Baptism for Salvation

The importance of Baptism is made manifest in the saying of the Lord Christ to Nicodemus, "Most assuredly, I say to you, unless one is born again, he cannot see the kingdom of God."[78] And He explained the meaning of this birth, responding to the question of Nicodemus, saying, "Most assuredly, I say to you, unless one is born of water and the Spirit, he cannot enter the kingdom of God."[79]

---

76   Luke 8:6, 13.
77   1 Timothy 4:1.
78   John 3:3.
79   John 3:5.

This is an explicit verse, meaning that without Baptism, a person cannot enter the kingdom of God, nor see it. And so salvation is through Baptism, for which faith paves the way.

And likewise, the Lord Christ said explicitly and clearly, "He who believes and is baptized will be saved."[80] And likewise also when He sent His disciples to spread His kingdom upon the earth, He said to them, "Go therefore and make disciples of all the nations, baptizing them in the name of the Father and of the Son and of the Holy Spirit, teaching them to observe all things that I have commanded you."[81] This verse shows that salvation requires faith that comes from discipleship, Baptism that is the direct door, and good works by observing the commandments. Had Baptism been unnecessary for salvation, it would have been sufficient for the Lord to say to His disciples, "Go and preach the faith," without mentioning Baptism.

Our teacher Paul the Apostle explains how salvation is [accomplished] through Baptism, and how it is the second birth, in his epistle to his disciple Titus, Bishop of Crete, by saying, "But when the kindness and the love of God our Savior toward man appeared, not by works of righteousness which we have done, but according to His mercy He saved us, through the washing of regeneration and renewing of the Holy Spirit."[82]

The Practice of Baptism from the Beginning

This principle that the Lord Christ founded—"He who believes and is baptized will be saved"[83]—was followed by the Church from the beginning. For on the Day of Pentecost, after Peter the Apostle had stood raising his voice with the word of faith, and the hearers were cut to the heart, "then Peter said to them, 'Repent, and let every one of you be baptized in the name of Jesus Christ for the remission of sins; and you shall receive the gift of the Holy

---

80   Mark 16:16.
81   Matthew 28:19–20.
82   Titus 3:4–5.
83   Mark 16:16.

Spirit.'"[84] This verse is explicit, in that there is remission of sins through Baptism. And how is a person saved without remission of their sins? Therefore, Baptism is necessary for the salvation of the person, for through it their sins are remitted, and through it [the person] is prepared to receive the Holy Spirit.

We receive the gift of the Holy Spirit in the second Mystery of the Mysteries of the Church: the Mystery of Holy Anointing or the Mystery of Myron. And the previous verse shows all these meanings.

On the Day of Pentecost, after St. Peter had spoken about Baptism, "then those who gladly received his word were baptized; and that day about three thousand souls were added to them."[85] Therefore, if faith alone saved a person, what would be the need for three thousand souls to be baptized in one day? How easy would it have been for the apostles to say to them, "As long as you have believed, brethren, you may go in peace.[86] This is enough. You have been saved, and the matter is all over!"

And likewise, we see that after the Ethiopian eunuch had believed through the hand of Philip, he immediately said to him, "What hinders me from being baptized?"[87] And so Philip went down with him into the water and baptized him, and he went on his way rejoicing. And the keeper of the prison in Philippi, who believed through the hands of Paul and Silas, "immediately he and all his family were baptized."[88]

Likewise is Cornelius also, to whom the angel of God appeared, saying to him, "Your prayers and your alms have come up for a memorial before God."[89] After St. Peter had spoken the word of life to him, and after the Holy Spirit had come upon all those who were hearing the word, "then Peter answered, 'Can anyone forbid water, that these should not be baptized who have received

---

84 Acts 2:38.
85 Acts 2:41.
86 Last phrase is literally "Go with the blessing of God."
87 Acts 8:36.
88 Acts 16:33.
89 Acts 10:4.

the Holy Spirit just as we have?' And he commanded them to be baptized in the name of the Lord."[90] Also Lydia, the seller of purple, when she believed through the hand of Paul the Apostle, "she and her household were baptized."[91]

How beautiful is the statement which St. Paul the Apostle said concerning Baptism, "For as many of you as were baptized into Christ have put on Christ."[92] Then in Baptism, a person puts on Christ. What salvation is greater than this! Baptism is the door through which a person enters into salvation, and faith is the preparation for it. This we say, because many of the Protestants think that faith is sufficient for a person to be saved, or they think that regeneration comes through faith and not through Baptism! They do not see that Baptism itself is the regeneration, despite how explicit the verse is: "Through the washing of regeneration."[93]

[This is] also despite the saying of the apostle in his epistle to the Ephesians: "Husbands, love your wives, just as Christ also loved the church and gave Himself for her, that He might sanctify and cleanse her with the washing of water by the word, that He might present her to Himself a glorious church, not having spot."[94] The Protestants, and those who follow them, claim that the phrase, "that He might sanctify and cleanse her with the washing of water by the word," means that He sanctifies her by the word, ignoring the phrase "the washing of water" as though it were meaningless.

Here, "the word" means the preaching. So, what does the phrase "the washing of water" mean? It means Baptism, to which a person reaches by the preaching, that is, by the word. And so the commandment of the Lord Christ applies: "Make disciples … baptizing them,"[95] making disciples by the word, and baptizing them with the washing of water.

---

90   Acts 10:47–48.
91   Acts 16:15.
92   Galatians 3:27.
93   Titus 3:5.
94   Ephesians 5:25–27.
95   Matthew 28:19.

The Theological Explanation of the Importance of Baptism

What is the essence of the Christian teaching on Baptism as a means for salvation? Why is it required for salvation? And why is it not possible for anyone to be saved without it? The matter is very clear, and the following is the explanation.

The Scriptures say, "The wages of sin is death."[96] Then death is necessary. Also, it is necessary that the way of salvation begins by death, and salvation continues by death, and the last stage of salvation comes by death. Salvation begins by death, and ends by death, and continues by death, because the wages of sin is death. So, what is the meaning of this word?

1. Salvation Began by Death

Salvation began by the death of Christ on the cross, where He paid the price of sin and purchased us by His blood. How does salvation reach you? It reaches you by death. And how is that? By His death, Christ granted salvation; and so that you may have a share in this salvation, you must partake with Christ of His death: you die with Christ, and you rise up with Christ, so that you may be glorified with Him. Therefore, Paul the Apostle says, "That I may know Him and the power of His resurrection, and the fellowship of His sufferings, being conformed to His death."[97]

Unless you enter into this death, the second death will befall you, that is, the eternal torment in the lake of fire.[98] And how do you enter into this death? How do you partake with Christ of His death? That is done through Baptism. For this reason, St. Paul the Apostle says, "Or do you not know that as many of us as were baptized into Christ Jesus were baptized into His death? Therefore we were buried with Him through baptism into death."[99]

Our death with Christ, and our burial with Him, is that which makes us partake with Him of the glories of His resurrection.

---

96   Romans 6:23.
97   Philippians 3:10.
98   See Revelation 20:14.
99   Romans 6:3–4.

St. Paul the Apostle, therefore, says, "For if we have been united together in the likeness of His death, certainly we also shall be in the likeness of His resurrection.... Now if we died with Christ, we believe that we shall also live with Him."[100]

The subject is summarized in the following:

The wages of sin is death. Therefore, man must die and be buried. Christ, however, died for us. And we ought to partake with Him of His death, so that we may not be far from the merits we receive through the death of Christ. We should not at all leave Christ to die alone for us, without partaking with Him of His death, or at least we should be conformed to His death. We enter "the fellowship of His sufferings, being conformed to His death."[101] And so did the apostle say, "[We] were baptized into His death.... we were buried with Him.... We have been united together in the likeness of His death ... our old man was crucified with Him.... Now if we died with Christ, we believe that we shall also live with Him."[102]

The Scriptures explained that this death is accomplished through Baptism. We are fully immersed in it, as though we were buried in the baptismal font, as St. Paul said, "We were buried with Him through baptism into death."[103] Then we rise up from this water "in newness of life,"[104] "knowing this, that our old man was crucified with Him, that the body of sin might be done away with."[105]

Baptism is then necessary for salvation, because it is fellowship in the death of Christ, because it is faith in death as a means for life, and [it is] confession that the wages of sin is death. Those who say that salvation is accomplished by merely having faith alone, without Baptism, have not yet understood what faith is. Therefore, let us discuss this matter together to understand it.

---

100 Romans 6:5, 8.
101 Philippians 3:10.
102 Romans 6:3–8.
103 Romans 6:4.
104 Ibid.
105 Romans 6:6.

What is faith? It is to believe that the wages of sin is death, and to believe that Christ died for you, and to believe that you must die with Him, to live with Him also; therefore, faith leads you to what we have said:

That salvation began by death, the death of Christ. This is the salvation whose price He paid; that we began to obtain this salvation by death, having died with Christ and been buried with Him through Baptism. This is the salvation which we received. We also say that this salvation continues by death.

2. Salvation Continues by Death

And so does St. Paul the Apostle say, "Likewise you also, reckon yourselves to be dead indeed to sin, but alive to God in Christ Jesus our Lord. Therefore do not let sin reign in your mortal body, that you should obey it in its lusts."[106]

This is a very beautiful word, fully explaining the Orthodox faith to us. "Do not let sin reign in your mortal body." We have entered salvation by death, and our body must continue to be a mortal [or dead] body to the worldly lusts. So long as it is mortal [or dead], then salvation courses in it. But if the lusts of the body began to arise from this death and to move, then we would be in danger of losing salvation, because salvation cannot be accomplished except by death.

Therefore, we pray to God in the litanies of the Ninth Hour, saying, "Put to death our carnal lusts, O Christ, our God, and deliver us." And perhaps this is the fulfillment of the saying of the Scriptures, "But if by the Spirit you put to death the deeds of the body, you will live."[107] Did not St. Paul the Apostle say, "Then death is working in us"[108]?

And so does St. Paul the Apostle say too, "For we who live are always delivered to death for Jesus' sake, that the life of Jesus also may be manifested in our mortal flesh."[109] And he said, "And if

---

106 Romans 6:11–12.
107 Romans 8:13.
108 2 Corinthians 4:12.
109 2 Corinthians 4:11.

Christ is in you, the body is dead because of sin, but the Spirit is life because of righteousness."[110] He also said, "For Your sake we are killed all day long; we are accounted as sheep for the slaughter."[111] And so we live "always carrying about in the body the dying of the Lord Jesus, that the life of Jesus also may be manifested in our body."[112]

Therefore, so long as we are walking in the path of salvation, the body must be dead to sin, and death must be working in us. A person who says that they are saved, while they love the world and the things in the world, is truly deceived, because "friendship with the world is enmity with God."[113] Salvation continues by death, death of the works of the body, death of the lusts of the body, death to the world and matter and its demands that war against the spirit.

What is the Meaning of "We Shall be Saved by His Life"?

Here, the following verse stands before us, which says, "For if when we were enemies we were reconciled to God through the death of His Son, much more, having been reconciled, we shall be saved by His life."[114] So, what is the meaning of "We shall be saved by His life"?

Its meaning is either that we are saved by His life as an Intercessor, as a Priest forever according to the order of Melchizedek, who "is also able to save to the uttermost those who come to God through Him, since He always lives to make intercession for them."[115] So we are saved by His life as an Intercessor, because we continually sin. And if we sin, "we have an Advocate with the Father, Jesus Christ the righteous."[116] We note here that the continual intercession of Christ for us means our continual need for salvation at all times and the continual work of salvation in us.

---

110 Romans 8:10.
111 Romans 8:36.
112 2 Corinthians 4:10.
113 James 4:4.
114 Romans 5:10.
115 Hebrews 7:25.
116 1 John 2:1.

Nevertheless, there is another beautiful meaning for the phrase "we shall be saved by His life": it is the saying of St. Paul the Apostle, "I have been crucified with Christ; it is no longer I who live, but Christ lives in me."[117] He says, "I have been crucified with Christ"; this is the death: "Crucifixion of the flesh with its passions and desires,"[118] as the apostle says. By this we are saved: when Christ is the one living in us. And the phrase "it is no longer I who live" means surrendering the will completely to the Lord, so that the person continually says, "Not my will, but Yours, be done." He is as though he were dead, non-existent, living not he, but Christ is the one living in him.

He says to Christ, "I am saved by Your death, and I am saved by Your life in me." This is the sound idea regarding salvation in the Orthodox understanding: we were saved by the death of Christ when we died with Him in Baptism. And we are also saved by the life of Christ in us, through our perfect submission to His will in our lives, saying with the apostle, "It is no longer I who live, but Christ lives in me."

3. Salvation is Fulfilled by Death

We said that salvation begins by death in Baptism, and it continues by death to the lusts of the world, so until when? The Scripture says, "Be faithful until death, and I will give you the crown of life."[119] And so death continues to work in you, until the body actually dies. So long as you are mortifying the works of the body, you are still walking in the path of salvation. When do you reach the end of the path? You reach it when you die and depart to the other world.

You are then still walking in the path. So do you stop halfway, crying out, "I have been saved"? Be humble, my brother, and listen to the saying of the apostle, "Considering the outcome of their conduct."[120] Do not boast in vain, for many began in the Spirit and [yet] finished in the flesh?

---

117 Galatians 2:20.
118 Cf. Galatians 5:24.
119 Revelation 2:10.
120 Hebrews 13:7.

We will present this subject in detail, God willing, when we speak about the fulfillment of salvation.

The Mysteries Required for Salvation

There are Mysteries that might not be necessary for you personally, for your salvation. For you might not get married, although you are a fruit of a marriage. And you might not suffer from a sickness in which you need the Mystery of the Anointing of the Sick. And you might not be ordained a priest, although you need the Mystery of the Priesthood, so that it presents to you the work of the Holy Spirit in the Mysteries necessary for you personally, for your salvation. For you undoubtedly require the Mystery of Baptism, of which we have spoken, and the Mystery of the Anointing of the Holy Spirit (Myron), and the Mystery of Repentance, and the Mystery of the Eucharist (Communion). Now we will speak about the importance of each of these Mysteries separately.

The Mystery of Holy Anointing

When St. Peter invited the Jews to Baptism, he said to them, "Repent, and let every one of you be baptized in the name of Jesus Christ for the remission of sins; and you shall receive the gift of the Holy Spirit."[121] So what is this gift of the Holy Spirit? And is it necessary in our life for salvation, and what is its importance? And can we be saved without it?

It is absolutely impossible for us to be saved without it, because our entire spiritual life is a response of our will to the work of the Holy Spirit within us. And if we do not receive the gift of the Holy Spirit, then our entire life is vain and lost. Regarding this grace, which we received from the Mystery of Holy Anointing, we continually cry out and say, "Your Holy Spirit do not take away from us," otherwise we perish.

---

121 Acts 2:38.

Your spiritual life does not at all depend on your human arm [alone]; rather, it is a fellowship with the Holy Spirit, as we will explain in the chapter about struggle and grace.

The Mystery of Holy Anointing is therefore necessary, of which St. John the Apostle spoke, saying, "But you have an anointing from the Holy One, and you know all things.... But the anointing which you have received from Him abides in you, and you do not need that anyone teach you; but as the same anointing teaches you concerning all things, and is true."[122]

To know the importance of the Holy Spirit for your salvation, we ask the following question: Can you have[123] a spiritual life without the work of the Holy Spirit within you? Can you walk in the path of salvation without the work of the Holy Spirit with you? It is impossible. Therefore, the anointing is necessary.

For this reason, the Apostles cared about the gift of the Holy Spirit to the believers, and in the beginning, they used to receive it through the laying on of the Apostles' hands, before Myron was used. We see this clearly in the story when Samaria received the faith, and it was considered complementary to faith and Baptism. The Scripture says:

> Now, when the apostles who were at Jerusalem heard that Samaria had received the word of God, they sent Peter and John to them, who, when they had come down, prayed for them that they might receive the Holy Spirit. For as yet He had fallen upon none of them. They had only been baptized in the name of the Lord Jesus. Then they laid hands on them, and they received the Holy Spirit.[124]

Then, Baptism was not sufficient for the people of Samaria, but it was necessary for them to receive the Holy Spirit.

The same word can also be said about the people of Ephesus when they believed. When St. Paul went there, he found disciples,

---

122 1 John 2:20, 27.
123 Literally: live.
124 Acts 8:14–17.

and he asked them, "'Did you receive the Holy Spirit when you believed?' So they said to him, 'We have not so much as heard whether there is a Holy Spirit.'"[125] For they were only baptized into John's baptism.[126] When St. Paul spoke to them, "They were baptized in the name of the Lord Jesus. And when Paul had laid hands on them, the Holy Spirit came upon them."[127]

Through Baptism, we partake with Christ of His death and receive the sonship. And through the Holy Spirit, we live a life befitting of us as sons. And both matters are necessary for our salvation.

The Mystery of the Eucharist—Communion

To realize the importance of the partaking of the body of the Lord and His blood, it is sufficient, out of conciseness, for us to mention the saying of Christ, "Most assuredly, I say to you, unless you eat the flesh of the Son of Man and drink His blood, you have no life in you. Whoever eats My flesh and drinks My blood has eternal life, and I will raise him up at the last day.... He who eats My flesh and drinks My blood abides in Me, and I in him."[128] Here we see that eternal life is connected with the partaking of the body of the Lord, in that whoever does not partake does not have life, that is, he perishes. Do you ask after this about the necessity of Communion for salvation?

If we are Orthodox and believe in the Orthodox faith, then we believe in what we say in the Divine Liturgy regarding the body of the Lord, which we partake of: "Given for us for salvation, remission of sins, and eternal life to those who partake of Him."[129] Does anyone ask the following question? "Is it possible to be saved without Communion?" I say, "No, it is not possible, because the body of the Lord is given for us for salvation, remission of sins, and eternal life to those who partake of Him."

---

125 Acts 19:2.
126 See Acts 19:3–4.
127 Acts 19:5–6.
128 John 6:53–56. See also John 6:57–58.
129 The Divine Liturgy According to St. Basil – The Confession.

How do we Explain This from the Theological Aspect?

In Baptism, you were saved from the Original Sin, and this is the first salvation you received. Baptism also made you a child of God and made you worthy to receive the merits we receive through the Blood. You, however, sin daily and need that your sin be erased by the Blood: "If we say that we have no sin, we deceive ourselves, and the truth is not in us."[130] You, then, sin daily and need the body of Christ, [which was] sacrificed for you. You need the holy sacrifice, a propitiation for your sins. And the holy sacrifice in the Mystery of the Eucharist is nothing but a continuation of the sacrifice of Christ. Therefore, it is not possible for you to be saved from your sins without it, this which is given for us for salvation and remission of sins. Through it, we also abide in the Lord, as He said.

Someone might come to you and say, "Do you want to be saved? Cast yourself at the feet of Christ and say to Him, 'Accept me, Jesus!'" These words, my brethren, require measures to be taken. Do you want to be accepted by Christ? There is a path for salvation through which He accepts you: you die with Christ and are buried with Him through Baptism, so He accepts you; you are anointed with [the anointing of] the Holy Spirit, so He accepts you; you partake of His body and drink His blood, so that you may abide in Him, and through this He accepts you; you confess your sins, so He accepts you; and so on. This is the practical path through which the Lord accepts you. But to ask Him to accept you, without walking in His path which He ordained, these words are not fitting.

The same thing we say about the phrase, "Surrender your life to Jesus!" How easy it is for a person to utter such words; how difficult, however, they are to be put into practice! Do you think that surrendering one's life is something easy? All our spiritual struggle is concentrated in this phrase, "Surrendering life." In it, a person surrenders their will to the Lord, surrenders their heart and emotions, surrenders their determination, surrenders their thoughts, and so on. That is to say, the person must do works befitting of repentance.

---

130 1 John 1:8.

And if we are speaking about the Mystery of the Eucharist, then we must precede it by speaking about the Mystery of Repentance.

The Mystery of Repentance

Is repentance necessary for salvation? Yes, without repentance, there is no salvation. You might be asking, "How is that? I believed, was baptized, and was justified." Yes, you were baptized, and you escaped from the Original Sin. But what about your actual sins that you commit daily? Where do you escape from them? And how do you escape from them?

After believing and being baptized, do faith and Baptism make you not fall into sin ever again? No, without a doubt. Look, John the Apostle decrees that "if we say that we have no sin, we deceive ourselves, and the truth is not in us."[131] This is because "no one is good but One, that is, God,"[132] "for we all stumble in many things."[133] And as we say in the Litany for the Departed, "For no one is pure and without blemish, even though his life on earth be a single day." Therefore, what do we say about all these sins? How is a person saved from them? Is it not through repentance?

Perhaps someone might whisper in your ear, saying, "Believe only—believe in the Lord Jesus, and you will be saved, you and your household."[134] This verse, my beloved brother, we said it in the past, before Baptism. But regarding your sins after Baptism, St. John the Apostle advises you concerning them, saying, "If we confess our sins, He is faithful and just to forgive us our sins and to cleanse us from all unrighteousness."[135] Regarding them, the Scripture says, "He who covers his sins will not prosper, but whoever confesses and forsakes them will have mercy."[136] For this reason, the holy Church has ordained for us the Mystery of Repentance.

---

131 1 John 1:8.
132 Matthew 19:17.
133 James 3:2.
134 See Acts 16:31.
135 1 John 1:9.
136 Proverbs 28:13.

So long as the believing person is prone to fall at all times, and prone to perish in their sin, despite their faith, and so long as the person is in a constant war against the sin in which they often slip, and stumble, and fall daily—God therefore ordained for us repentance, through which we may be renewed and cleansed and washed of our sin. And repentance is a work, whose importance and necessity no one of the Protestants denies. And in repentance, regret, mourning, confession, and determination to leave sin are included, and all of these are works.

I do not say that through repentance alone a person is saved; for repentance without the blood of Christ is futile. I say, however, that repentance makes a person worthy to be washed and cleansed by the blood of Christ, and so they are saved. The blood of Christ is like a great treasure, but we approach it through repentance, and we take of it and are enriched. But if we do not use repentance, then the treasure maintains its value, and we remain far from it, poor, perishing of hunger. The tenderness of the father is present, and the new garment is present, the fatted calf is present, but the prodigal son must approach the father through repentance, so that he may obtain all these. Let us confess, then, that "God has also granted to the Gentiles repentance to life."[137]

The importance of repentance is made clear by the saying of the Lord Christ—glory be to Him—"Unless you repent you will all likewise perish."[138] This verse indicates that repentance is a means of salvation, delivering from perdition, and it also indicates that without repentance, the sinful person perishes. "Truly, these times of ignorance God overlooked, but now commands all men everywhere to repent."[139] Not only must they repent, but also this must be followed by them doing "works befitting repentance."[140]

This repentance is proclaimed by the holy Apostles as a means of salvation from the perdition prepared for sinners. For St. Peter the Apostle says about God, that He "is longsuffering toward

---

137 Acts 11:18.
138 Luke 13:3.
139 Acts 17:30.
140 Acts 26:20.

us, not willing that any should perish but that all should come to repentance."[141] For here is a contrast between repentance and perdition, meaning that whoever comes to repentance is saved from—and escapes—perdition, and vice versa.

And St. Paul the Apostle explains the wrath prepared for the unrepentant, who are subject to the righteous judgment of God, saying, "Or do you despise the riches of His goodness, forbearance, and longsuffering, not knowing that the goodness of God leads you to repentance? But in accordance with your hardness and your impenitent heart you are treasuring up for yourself wrath in the day of wrath and revelation of the righteous judgment of God, who 'will render to each one according to his deeds.'"[142]

God did not ask for this repentance from the Gentiles only and from the unbelievers, but he asked for it in the Book of Revelation from the angels of the churches of Asia. He said to the angel of the church of Ephesus, "Remember therefore from where you have fallen; repent and do the first works, or else I will come to you quickly and remove your lampstand from its place—unless you repent."[143] He also asked for repentance from the angel of the church of Pergamos.[144] And He said to the angel of the church of Sardis, "Remember therefore how you have received and heard; hold fast and repent. Therefore if you will not watch, I will come upon you as a thief, and you will not know what hour I will come upon you."[145] He also said to the angel of the church of the Laodiceans, "Therefore be zealous and repent."[146]

Do not suppose, my brother, that Adam's sin alone was that which was deserving of death, but rather, generally, the wages of sin is death. Every sin you commit after your Baptism could be a reason for your perdition—unless you repent.

The Mystery of Repentance in the Church is also called the

---

141 2 Peter 3:9.
142 Romans 2:4–6.
143 Revelation 2:5.
144 See Revelation 2:16.
145 Revelation 3:3.
146 Revelation 3:19.

Mystery of Confession. You need to come and confess your sins, so that you may receive an absolution for them from the priest, and so they are forgiven you. And the holy Church has practiced the Mystery of Confession from the beginning. For in the time of the Apostles, the Scripture says, "And many who had believed came confessing and telling their deeds."[147] Even before the Apostles, the Scripture says about John the Baptist: "[They] were baptized by him in the Jordan, confessing their sins."[148]

On the path of your salvation, then, I wish that you benefit from the saying of the Lord Christ to His disciples: "Receive the Holy Spirit. If you forgive the sins of any, they are forgiven them; if you retain the sins of any, they are retained."[149]

Good Works

We have now spoken about salvation by the blood of Christ, and how the merit we receive by the blood of Christ requires faith, Baptism, the Mystery of the Holy Anointing, the Mystery of Repentance, and the Mystery of the Eucharist. It remains for us to speak about works and their place in the matter of salvation. We have devoted a special chapter to this topic because of its importance.

---

147 Acts 19:18.
148 Matthew 3:6.
149 John 20:22–23.

CHAPTER TWO

The Importance of Works
in the Subject of Salvation

Introduction

The works of a person are either good or evil. The evil works destroy a person and make them lose their salvation. The good works, however, are necessary for salvation. Their absence indicates that faith is dead and that it has no fruit. Good works alone, however, are not sufficient for salvation, without faith, Baptism, and the merits we receive through the blood of Christ.

These good works are the fruits of faith, and a proof of the existence of faith, and through them we complete the faith, as we will explain in detail later. Also, God has asked for these good works and has commanded that they be done, and He has decreed punishments on those who neglect them. There will be judgment on the Last Day according to works.

Salvation is not accomplished because of the good works; neither is it accomplished without them. For salvation is not [accomplished] except by the blood of Christ alone, but works qualify [a person] to be worthy of this blood. Nevertheless, we need to draw attention to a very important matter: that is, a person's good works need the assistance of grace. For Christ—glory be to Him—said, "Without Me you can do nothing."[150] Therefore, our good works are the result of the participation of our will with the work of the Holy Spirit in us.

---

150 John 15:5.

The texts of the Holy Scriptures that [appear to] diminish the value of works mean one of the following. They either mean the works of the Law, like circumcision, ritualistic practices, keeping the days and months and feasts, and so on. Or they may mean to attack the works that are not founded on the blood of Christ and His redemption, such as the works of the unbelievers and Pagans, and so on. Or they may mean works without faith, or works prior to faith. We will try to treat all these points, one by one, according to the assistance that is granted by the grace of the Lord.

Evil Works Lead to Perdition

This is a natural thing. For God, as He is perfect in His mercy, so is He also perfect in His justice. And so long as "the wages of sin is death,"[151] then the sinner must receive punishment for their sin. It is true that Christ died for us, but no one enjoys the merit of the death of Christ, except the repentant, otherwise this free salvation would be an open door for heedlessness and corruption, and a declaration of committing sin without fear of its punishment, relying on the blood of Christ and His propitiation that had paid in full for everything!

Therefore, St. Paul the Apostle says in this context, "What shall we say then? Shall we continue in sin that grace may abound? Certainly not! How shall we who died to sin live any longer in it?... Therefore do not let sin reign in your mortal body, that you should obey it in its lusts."[152] St. Paul the Apostle continues his speech, saying, "What then? Shall we sin because we are not under law but under grace? Certainly not! Do you not know that to whom you present yourselves slaves to obey, you are that one's slaves whom you obey, whether of sin leading to death, or of obedience leading to righteousness?"[153]

In these two verses, the Apostle showed us that if we obeyed sin while we are under grace, then the obedience would be to death.

---

151 Romans 6:23.
152 Romans 6:1–2, 12.
153 Romans 6:15–16.

And so long as it is to death, then it means our loss of eternal life, which is ours in Christ Jesus.

How important these verses are, especially that they are the words of inspiration on the tongue of Paul the Apostle, who is the greatest Apostle whom the Protestants depend on, regarding the subject of grace and the justification by faith; also because they are verses from the epistle to the Romans, which is the first and fundamental epistle, on which they depend in this subject.[154]

Other Texts from the Epistles of Paul the Apostle

Numerous are the Scriptures that indicate that evil works lead to perdition:

✤ "Now the works of the flesh are evident, which are: adultery, fornication, uncleanness, lewdness, idolatry, sorcery, hatred, contentions, jealousies, outbursts of wrath, selfish ambitions, dissensions, heresies, envy, murders, drunkenness, revelries, and the like; of which I tell you beforehand, just as I also told you in time past, that those who practice such things will not inherit the kingdom of God."[155] Faith, then, with such evil works, benefits nothing and does not alone save a person.

✤ "For this you know, that no fornicator, unclean person, nor covetous man, who is an idolater, has any inheritance in the kingdom of Christ and God. Let no one deceive you with empty words, for because of these things the wrath of God comes upon the sons of disobedience."[156]

✤ "Do you not know that the unrighteous will not inherit the kingdom of God? Do not be deceived. Neither fornicators, nor idolaters, nor adulterers, nor homosexuals, nor sodomites, nor thieves, nor covetous, nor drunkards, nor revilers, nor extortioners will inherit the kingdom of God."[157]

---

154 See also Galatians 2:17.
155 Galatians 5:19–21.
156 Ephesians 5:5–6.
157 1 Corinthians 6:9–10.

✣ "But fornicators and adulterers God will judge."[158]

These are explicit verses, in which St. Paul the Apostle presents more than twenty works that shut the kingdom of God before the believer if they sin. St. Paul the Apostle—the Apostle of grace and justification—also speaks very forcefully in his epistle to the Hebrews, saying:

✣ "For if we sin willfully after we have received the knowledge of the truth, there no longer remains a sacrifice for sins, but a certain fearful expectation of judgment, and fiery indignation which will devour the adversaries."[159]

✣ "Of how much worse punishment, do you suppose, will he be thought worthy who has trampled the Son of God underfoot, counted the blood of the covenant by which he was sanctified a common thing, and insulted the Spirit of grace? For we know Him who said, 'Vengeance is Mine, I will repay,' says the Lord. And again, 'The LORD will judge His people.' It is a fearful thing to fall into the hands of the living God."[160]

He also fiercely says what resembles the same meaning that is in the first two verses [Hebrews 10:26–27] on another subject of the epistle to the Hebrews (6:4–8).

✣ "For the wrath of God is revealed from heaven against all ungodliness and unrighteousness of men."[161]

✣ "Therefore put to death your members which are on the earth: fornication, uncleanness, passion, evil desire, and covetousness, which is idolatry. Because of these things the wrath of God is coming upon the sons of disobedience."[162]

✣ "Taking vengeance on those who do not know God, and on those who do not obey the gospel of our Lord Jesus Christ. These shall be punished with everlasting destruction from

---

158 Hebrews 13:4.
159 Hebrews 10:26–27.
160 Hebrews 10:29–31.
161 Romans 1:18.
162 Colossians 3:5–6.

the presence of the Lord."[163] We note here that He made the everlasting destruction [as] a punishment for two matters together: abandoning the faith and abandoning works. For the phrase "those who do not know God" concerns a lack of faith, and the phrase "those who do not obey the gospel" concerns abandoning works.

✛ "But to those who are self-seeking and do not obey the truth, but obey unrighteousness—indignation and wrath, tribulation and anguish, on every soul of man who does evil, of the Jew first and also of the Greek; but glory, honor, and peace to everyone who works what is good, to the Jew first and also to the Greek."[164] Here we note not only the punishment for evil works, but also the reward for good works.

Comment: We have previously quoted verses on the punishment of sin, and how the believer, if they sin, perishes in their sin; that evil works prevents the one who has sinned from inheriting the kingdom of God; the wrath of God befalls them; they are considered of the sons of disobedience; they meet a fearful judgment; fiery indignation will devour them; they are punished with everlasting destruction from the presence of the Lord; tribulation and anguish will befall their soul; God will judge them.

All these were said by St. Paul the Apostle, the one who spoke extensively about grace and justification by faith. We have begun and mentioned these verses, so that in their light we may understand the verses of grace and faith that were said by St. Paul himself, and that it may not seem to anyone that St. Paul the Apostle teaches otherwise, but he himself also taught—in nearly every epistle— that sins shut the kingdom of heaven. He also taught that evil works annul the work of faith. For he said in his epistle to Titus:

✛ "They profess to know God, but in works they deny Him, being abominable, disobedient, and disqualified for every good work."[165]

---

163 2 Thessalonians 1:8–9.
164 Romans 2:8–10.
165 Titus 1:16.

Other Texts Besides the Epistles of St. Paul the Apostle

✛ "For if God did not spare the angels who sinned, but cast them down to hell and delivered them into chains of darkness, to be reserved for judgment; and did not spare the ancient world... then the Lord knows how to deliver the godly out of temptations and to reserve the unjust under punishment for the day of judgment, and especially those who walk according to the flesh in the lust of uncleanness.... [These] will utterly perish in their own corruption, and will receive the wages of unrighteousness.... for whom is reserved the blackness of darkness forever.... For if, after they have escaped the pollutions of the world through the knowledge of the Lord and Savior Jesus Christ, they are again entangled in them and overcome, the latter end is worse for them than the beginning. For it would have been better for them not to have known the way of righteousness, than having known it, to turn from the holy commandment delivered to them. But it has happened to them according to the true proverb: 'A dog returns to his own vomit,' and, 'a sow, having washed, to her wallowing in the mire.'"[166]

It is clear from the last verses that he is speaking about believers who perish.

✛ "What will be the end of those who do not obey the gospel of God? Now 'If the righteous one is scarcely saved, where will the ungodly and the sinner appear?'"[167]

✛ "Then Peter said to her, 'How is it that you have agreed together to test the Spirit of the Lord? Look, the feet of those who have buried your husband are at the door, and they will carry you out.' Then immediately she fell down at his feet and breathed her last. And the young men came in and found her dead, and carrying her out, buried her by her husband."[168]

The death of Ananias and Sapphira is a proof that an evil work

---

166 2 Peter 2:4–22.
167 1 Peter 4:17–18.
168 Acts 5:9–10.

leads to perdition, and that faith alone is not sufficient. For both of them were believers in Christ, but their hearts were not upright, so they perished. The Scripture says that, after their death, "great fear came upon all the church and upon all who heard these things."[169]

✤ "But the cowardly, unbelieving, abominable, murderers, sexually immoral, sorcerers, idolaters, and all liars shall have their part in the lake which burns with fire and brimstone, which is the second death."[170]

✤ "In the measure that she glorified herself and lived luxuriously, in the same measure give her torment and sorrow."[171]

✤ "Whoever hates his brother is a murderer, and you know that no murderer has eternal life abiding in him."[172]

✤ "My brethren, let not many of you become teachers, knowing that we shall receive a stricter judgment. For we all stumble in many things."[173]

✤ "Come now, you rich, weep and howl for your miseries that are coming upon you!... Do not grumble against one another, brethren, lest you be condemned. Behold, the Judge is standing at the door!"[174]

Comment: We saw in the previous texts [from the Scriptures] that many sins cause perdition, cast [people] into the lake which burns with fire and brimstone, bring torment and sorrow, deprive [a person] of eternal life, cast into misery and condemnation; whether the sins that seem grave, or the sins that are disdained by some, such as much teaching, excessive luxury, wronging the hirelings, hating one's brother, and so on. And this matter is the teaching of the Lord Christ Himself:

✤ "For the hour is coming in which all who are in the graves will hear His voice and come forth—those who have done good, to

---

169 Acts 5:11.
170 Revelation 21:8.
171 Revelation 18:7.
172 1 John 3:15.
173 James 3:1–2.
174 James 5:1, 9.

the resurrection of life, and those who have done evil, to the resurrection of condemnation."[175]

✤ "Therefore as the tares are gathered and burned in the fire, so it will be at the end of this age. The Son of Man will send out His angels, and they will gather out of His kingdom all things that offend, and those who practice lawlessness, and will cast them into the furnace of fire. There will be wailing and gnashing of teeth."[176]

✤ "Every tree that does not bear good fruit is cut down and thrown into the fire. Therefore by their fruits you will know them."[177]

In all the previous texts, we note that He did not talk about casting the unbelievers into fire or condemnation, rather "those who have done evil," "all things that offend, and those who practice lawlessness," and the one "that does not bear good fruit."

The following verses clearly show that faith alone benefits nothing for salvation if it is not accompanied by good works.

✤ "Not everyone who says to Me, 'Lord, Lord,' shall enter the kingdom of heaven, but he who does the will of My Father in heaven. Many will say to Me in that day, 'Lord, Lord, have we not prophesied in Your name, cast out demons in Your name, and done many wonders in Your name?' And then I will declare to them, 'I never knew you; depart from Me, you who practice lawlessness!'"[178]

In these verses, we note that those who were perishing were not only believers, but they also possessed gifts and performed miracles.

✤ "Then He will also say to those on the left hand, Depart from Me, you cursed, into the everlasting fire prepared for the devil and his angels: for I was hungry and you gave Me no food; I was thirsty and you gave Me no drink; I was a stranger and you

---

175 John 5:28–29.
176 Matthew 13:40–42.
177 Matthew 7:19–20.
178 Matthew 7:21–23.

did not take Me in, naked and you did not clothe Me, sick and in prison and you did not visit Me.' Then they also will answer Him, saying, 'Lord, when….' And these will go away into everlasting punishment, but the righteous into eternal life."[179]

Here we note that those who were perishing were not murderers, adulterers, or idolaters. However, just not feeding the hungry—and just not visiting the sick—was a reason for their perdition.

✤ "Unless you repent you will all likewise perish."[180]

✤ "If your right eye causes you to sin, pluck it out and cast it from you; for it is more profitable for you that one of your members perish, than for your whole body to be cast into hell. And if your right hand causes you to sin…"[181]

Here, the reason for being cast into hell was not unbelief [the lack of faith], but one of the sins of the flesh, such as the lust of the eye that leads to adultery, or stealing.

✤ "Strive to enter through the narrow gate, for many, I say to you, will seek to enter and will not be able. When once the Master of the house has risen up and shut the door, and you begin to stand outside and knock at the door, saying, 'Lord, Lord, open for us,' … But He will say, 'I tell you I do not know you, where you are from. Depart from Me, all you workers of iniquity.' There will be weeping and gnashing of teeth."[182]

Here, He is speaking to believers who say to Him, "Lord, Lord," but they perished because they were workers of iniquity.

✤ "It is easier for a camel to go through the eye of a needle than for a rich man to enter the kingdom of God."[183]

That is to say, there are people who will lose the kingdom, not because of their lack of faith, but because of the dangers of wealth.

✤ "But I say to you that for every idle word men may speak,

---

179 Matthew 25:41–46.
180 Luke 13:3, 5.
181 Matthew 5:29–30.
182 Luke 13:24–28.
183 Matthew 19:24.

they will give account of it in the day of judgment. For by your words you will be justified, and by your words you will be condemned."[184]

A person's faith does not prevent them from falling into condemnation because of their words. Here we are reminded of the saying of our teacher St. Basil the Great: "What do all other righteous actions avail me if I am to be liable to hell-fire because I called my brother 'fool'?"[185] For our Lord Jesus Christ says, "Whoever says, 'You fool!' shall be in danger of hell fire."[186]

Judgment According to Works

This is a clear truth that shows the importance of the works of a person.

In the Old Testament, David says in the psalm, "Also to You, O Lord, belongs mercy; for You render to each one according to his work."[187] And the Book of Ecclesiastes says, "For God will bring every work into judgment, including every secret thing, whether good or evil."[188]

In the New Testament, this truth was confirmed from the mouth of the Lord Christ and the mouths of His holy Apostles. On this, the Master Lord said, "For the Son of Man will come in the glory of His Father with His angels, and then He will reward each according to his works."[189] He also said, "For the hour is coming in which all who are in the graves will hear His voice and come forth—those who have done good, to the resurrection of life, and those who have done evil, to the resurrection of condemnation."[190] Note that in this verse, He is speaking about works: "Those who

---

184 Matthew 12:36–37.
185 Saint Basil, *Ascetical Works*, Wagner M.M., trans. (Washington, DC: The Catholic University of America Press, 1962), 226.
186 Matthew 5:22.
187 Psalms 62:12.
188 Ecclesiastes 12:14.
189 Matthew 16:27.
190 John 5:28–29.

have done good ... and those who have done evil."

Condemnation is not only on works, but even on words. Therefore, He said, "For by your words you will be justified, and by your words you will be condemned."[191]

This matter is clear in the Book of Revelation, for the Lord sent to each angel of the angels of the seven churches, saying to him, "I know your works."[192] The Lord also said explicitly, "And behold, I am coming quickly, and My reward is with Me, to give to every one according to his work."[193] In this Book, it was said, "Blessed are the dead who die in the Lord from now on. 'Yes,' says the Spirit, 'that they may rest from their labors, and their works follow them.'"[194]

The picture of the Judgment that the Lord Jesus explained to us, concerning His words that He would say to those on His right hand, and His words to those on His left hand, is a picture of a judgment according to works. For He said to those on His right hand, "For I was hungry and you gave Me food; I was thirsty and you gave Me drink; I was a stranger and you took Me in..." and based on these good works, He said to them, "Come, you blessed of My Father, inherit the kingdom prepared for you from the foundation of the world." Likewise did He do with the wicked, judging them according to their works.[195]

Then it is sufficient for a person to lose the kingdom if they neglect to feed the hungry or visit the sick, their heart being devoid of this mercy, no matter how much faith they have; and no matter how much hollow confidence they have in themselves, it will not benefit them at all! How serious is the saying of our teacher James the Apostle: "What does it profit, my brethren, if someone says he has faith but does not have works? Can faith save him?"[196]

The judgment being according to works is a truth of which

---

191 Matthew 12:37.
192 Revelation 2:2.
193 Revelation 22:12.
194 Revelation 14:13.
195 See Matthew 25:31–46.
196 James 2:14.

St. Paul the Apostle spoke abundantly. He said, "For we must all appear before the judgment seat of Christ, that each one may receive the things done in the body, according to what he has done, whether good or bad."[197] He also said, "But in accordance with your hardness and your impenitent heart you are treasuring up for yourself wrath in the day of wrath and revelation of the righteous judgment of God, who 'will render to each one according to his deeds.'"[198]

As a summary of the judgment according to works, St. Paul the Apostle also said, "For whatever a man sows, that he will also reap. For he who sows to his flesh will of the flesh reap corruption, but he who sows to the Spirit will of the Spirit reap everlasting life."[199] He also said, "Each one's work will become clear; for the Day will declare it, because it will be revealed by fire; and the fire will test each one's work, of what sort it is."[200] And he also said, "Each one will receive his own reward according to his own labor,"[201] and did not say, "according to his own faith," nor, "according to grace."

On the judgment according to works, St. Peter the Apostle said about the Father: "Who without partiality judges according to each one's work, conduct yourselves throughout the time of your stay here in fear."[202]

If works were of such a degree of gravity—whether good or evil—so that a person is judged on their basis, does anyone dare diminish the value of works and their importance? If God does not forget "a cup of cold water,"[203] so that he shall not lose his reward, and He never forgets the labor of love, "therefore, my beloved brethren, be steadfast, immovable, always abounding in the work of the Lord, knowing that your labor is not in vain in the Lord."[204]

---

197 2 Corinthians 5:10.
198 Romans 2:5–7.
199 Galatians 6:7–8.
200 1 Corinthians 3:13.
201 1 Corinthians 3:8.
202 1 Peter 1:17.
203 Matthew 10:42.
204 1 Corinthians 15:58.

Works are very important on the path of our salvation and important in determining our eternal fate; therefore, let us then consider how necessary they are.

Works are a Necessary Fruits of the Faith

Works are fruits of the faith. The living faith must bear fruit, that is, good works. These works are proof of the presence of faith and its viability. They are also fruits of the work of the Holy Spirit in us, and they are necessary fruits for the life of repentance that we live. Does God seek these works, or does He seek these fruits? Yes, He does seek them, and He emphasizes that.

St. John the Baptist stood, crying out and saying, "Therefore bear fruits worthy of repentance, and do not begin to say to yourselves, 'We have Abraham as our father.'"[205] [The fact] that God chose you does not mean that you are saved without works. You must bear fruits worthy of repentance. What if we do not bear [fruits]? If you do not bear fruit, then your end is perdition. What is the proof of this?

St. John the Baptist—the greatest of those born of women—continues and says, "And even now the ax is laid to the root of the trees. Therefore every tree which does not bear good fruit is cut down and thrown into the fire."[206] That is, the one who does not do good works perishes. You might protest, saying, "Abraham is my father. I am born of God. I am justified, and sanctified, and renewed." I say to you, "Bear fruits worthy of repentance!"

These words are not only said by St. John the Baptist, but in the New Testament we find St. Paul the Apostle say, "[I] declared first to those in Damascus and in Jerusalem, and throughout all the region of Judea, and then to the Gentiles, that they should repent, turn to God, and do works befitting repentance."[207]

And in his epistle to Titus, he says, "This is a faithful saying,

---

205 Luke 3:8.
206 Luke 3:9.
207 Acts 26:20.

and these things I want you to affirm constantly, that those who have believed in God should be careful to maintain good works."[208] Why is this, O great saint? Our teacher Paul continues his word, saying, "And let our people also learn to maintain good works ... that they may not be unfruitful."[209] Works then are the fruits of faith. If you have faith, and it does not bear fruit, then it is a dead faith. For if it were living, it would bear fruit.

This issue our teacher James the Apostle extensively explains, saying, "What does it profit, my brethren, if someone says he has faith but does not have works? Can faith save him?"[210] You believe in Christ and say, "He has cleansed me, renewed me, and justified me." This is very good. But if you do not have works, can this faith save you? James the Apostle very explicitly confirms the inability of faith to save the person who has no works.

Was St. James the Apostle the only one who attacked such a dead faith? No, even St. Paul the Apostle also said, "Though I have all faith, so that I could remove mountains, but have not love, I am nothing."[211]

If you are truly a son of God and a temple of God, and the Holy Spirit lives in you, then you must have works that are the fruits of the Spirit in you. Our teacher Paul the Apostle explains these fruits, saying, "But the fruit of the Spirit is love, joy, peace, longsuffering, kindness, goodness, faithfulness, gentleness, self-control."[212] Are these fruits present in you? If they are not present, then what is the proof that the Holy Spirit works in you?

The tree that does not bear fruit is a dead tree. And the Lord Christ—glory be to Him—said, "Every tree that does not bear good fruit is cut down and thrown into the fire. Therefore by their fruits you will know them. Not everyone who says to Me, 'Lord, Lord,' shall enter the kingdom of heaven, but he who does the

---

208 Titus 3:8.
209 Titus 3:14.
210 James 2:14.
211 1 Corinthians 13:2.
212 Galatians 5:22–23.

will of My Father in heaven."[213] Here we see that the Master Lord linked salvation and the good fruit, to which doing the will of the Father points.

And because of the importance of these fruits, the Lord said in His rebuke against the Jews, "Therefore I say to you, the kingdom of God will be taken from you and given to a nation bearing the fruits of it."[214]

The Lord has explained to us how He was determined to cut down the fig tree that did not bear fruit, and then the vinedresser entreated Him, saying, "Sir, let it alone this year also, until I dig around it and fertilize it. And if it bears fruit, well. But if not, after that you can cut it down."[215] Therefore, if you, brother, fear for yourself from this cutting down, then hasten now and do works worthy of the sons of God. Do not disdain the value of works, for the ax is laid to the root of the tree. Not only are works fruits of faith, but they are also more than that.

Works are a Proof of the Existence of Faith

St. James the Apostle says, "Show me your faith without your works, and I will show you my faith by my works."[216] That is, works indicate the existence of faith. And this is clear from the saying of the Scripture, "You will know them by their fruits.... Every good tree bears good fruit, but a bad tree bears bad fruit."[217]

Works are a Proof of Being Born of God

This is because the Scripture says, "If you know that He is righteous, you know that everyone who practices righteousness is born of Him."[218] It also says, "Whoever has been born of God does

---

213 Matthew 7:19–21.
214 Matthew 21:43.
215 Luke 13:6–9.
216 James 2:18.
217 Matthew 7:16–17.
218 1 John 2:29.

not sin."[219] And he considered this to be the characteristic of the children of God, for he says after it, "In this the children of God and the children of the devil are manifest."[220]

This also resembles what the Lord said to the Jews who were vainly boasting of their being sons of Abraham, "If you were Abraham's children, you would do the works of Abraham."[221] So He took works [as] a proof of sonship. St. Paul the Apostle also defended this point, saying, "For as many as are led by the Spirit of God, these are sons of God."[222]

If the children of God are those who are righteous, then what do we call the sinners? The Scriptures called them "Brood of vipers!"[223] and called them "the children of the devil,"[224] and also called them "the sons of disobedience,"[225] and, "children of wrath."[226]

If someone comes to you, then, and says to you, "I am a son of God, because I have been renewed, and justified, and sanctified." Say to him, "You will know them by their fruits." Works, then, are the fruits of faith, and a proof for the existence of faith, and a proof for being children of God. What else?

By Works, Faith is Perfected

For so does the Apostle say, "By works faith was made perfect."[227] For St. James the Apostle, when speaking about religion, the matter has come to the point that he said, "Pure and undefiled religion before God and the Father is this: to visit orphans and widows in their trouble, and to keep oneself unspotted from the world."[228] And all of these are works, without a doubt. Nevertheless, we do

---

219 1 John 3:9.
220 1 John 3:10.
221 John 8:39.
222 Romans 8:14.
223 Matthew 3:7.
224 1 John 3:10. Also see John 8:44.
225 Ephesians 2:2.
226 Ephesians 2:3.
227 James 2:22.
228 James 1:27.

not exploit this verse—as some do—and this is because we believe in the principle of the danger of using "the single verse."

So long as works have such importance, then, let us always remember the saying of St. James, "To him who knows to do good and does not do it, to him it is sin."[229]

The Importance of Conduct and Good Works

Some say, "What does salvation have to do with a person's conduct? The matter is a matter of faith, and not a matter of conduct or good works!" Therefore, we will demonstrate here the importance of conduct and the keeping of the commandments.

St. John the Apostle says, "If we say that we have fellowship with Him, and walk in darkness, we lie and do not practice the truth. But if we walk in the light as He is in the light, we have fellowship with one another, and the blood of Jesus Christ His Son cleanses us from all sin."[230] Then our walking[231] in the light has two results: fellowship and cleansing. Our walking in the light gives us fellowship with the Lord and with each other, as opposed to our walking in darkness, which suspends our fellowship with God.

Our walking in the light makes us worthy to be cleansed by the blood of Christ. For he says, "If we walk in the light ... the blood of Jesus Christ His Son cleanses us from all sin." "Walking in the light" here is a condition. Then the merits we receive through redemption and the cleansing by the blood of Christ require of us that we walk in the light. How important, then, this walking is, and how serious.

This good conduct [or walking] delivers us from the condemnation on the last day. The Scripture says, "There is therefore now no condemnation to those who are in Christ Jesus, who do not walk according to the flesh, but according to the Spirit."[232] In Christ Jesus, you are delivered from the condemnation, but with a condition: that your conduct be spiritual.

229 James 4:17.
230 1 John 1:6–7.
231 Or: conduct.
232 Romans 8:1.

We note here that the statement of St. Paul the Apostle includes both sides, the positive and the negative. On the one hand, the believer must stay away from evil, not walking according to the flesh. And on the other hand, they must bear fruit in [the life of] virtue, so they are walking according to the Spirit.

Therefore, how abundant are the commandments of our fathers, the Apostles, about the importance of conduct. St. Paul says in his epistle to the Galatians, "If we live in the Spirit, let us also walk in the Spirit."[233] He emphasizes this point, saying, "Walk in the Spirit, and you shall not fulfill the lust of the flesh."[234] And he commands that we should "walk in newness of life."[235]

And he sent to the Ephesians, saying, "I, therefore, the prisoner of the Lord, beseech you to walk worthy of the calling with which you were called."[236] He also says to them, "See then that you walk circumspectly, not as fools but as wise."[237]

Consequently, our fathers, the Apostles, forbade mixing with those who walk in a disorderly manner. Therefore, St. Paul says, "But we command you, brethren, in the name of our Lord Jesus Christ, that you withdraw from every brother who walks disorderly and not according to the tradition which he received from us."[238]

Our fathers, the Apostles, see that good conduct is a sign of love and a proof of abiding in Christ. Therefore, St. John the Apostle says, "This is love, that we walk according to His commandments."[239] And he also says, "He who says he abides in Him ought himself also to walk just as He walked."[240]

Also, keeping the commandments is a proof of the love of Christ and the relationship with Him. St. John the Apostle says,

---

233 Galatians 5:25.
234 Galatians 5:16.
235 Romans 6:4.
236 Ephesians 4:1.
237 Ephesians 5:15. See also 1 Thessalonians 2:12, 4:1; Colossians 1:10; Romans 13:13.
238 2 Thessalonians 3:6. See also 2 Thessalonians 3:11.
239 2 John 6.
240 1 John 2:6.

"For this is the love of God, that we keep His commandments."[241] And perhaps this is that which the Lord Himself said, "He who has My commandments and keeps them, it is he who loves Me."[242] As for it being a proof of the relationship with Him, the Lord has also said, "For whoever does the will of My Father in heaven is My brother and sister and mother."[243]

If the conduct of a person is so important that our fellowship with God and the Church depends on it, that our cleansing from sins by the blood of Christ depends on it, and our condemnation is through it; also that it is a proof of our love for God, and of our abiding in Him, and of our relationship with Him; therefore, is it right for someone to ignore it, saying that our life is not a matter of conduct, but of faith?

---

241 1 John 5:3.
242 John 14:21.
243 Matthew 12:50.

CHAPTER THREE

Struggle and Grace

If works are necessary for salvation, is a person saved by his works or by the grace of the Holy Spirit working with him? Many have gone to extremes in being fanatical about one of the two sides, thereby falling into error. We will try in this area to answer this important question: how is a person saved? By struggling, or by grace, or by both of them together?

Struggle and Grace Together

A person cannot be saved by their own struggle alone. For the Lord Christ—glory be to Him—said, "Without Me you can do nothing."[244] Therefore, your human arm alone, without the assistance of God, cannot save you, no matter how much you have struggled and labored.

Also, grace alone does not wish to save you, without the response of your will to it. How beautiful is the saying of St. John Chrysostom[245] that God does not desire that we be lying on our backs while He gives us the kingdom; therefore, grace does not do everything on its own. For it is not a means for laziness, negligence, and slackness.

---

244 John 15:5.
245 See for example St. John Chrysostom, *Homilies on the Epistle to the Romans* 18. (NPNF[1] 11): "For grace, though it be grace, saves the willing, not those who will not have it, and turn away from it, who persist in fighting against it, and opposing themselves to it." [Footnote by translator].

Do not, therefore, sit idly, without struggling in your life, saying, out of lack of understanding, "I leave myself to grace, to do whatever it wishes with me!" The work of grace in you, my brother, does not mean that you sleep and be negligent in performing your duties.

The Example of Joshua and Moses

Joshua the son of Nun was leading the army and fighting against Amalek, and at the same time Moses the prophet was standing on the top of the hill, lifting his hands in prayer.[246] So, were the people victorious through the army of Joshua the warrior, or through the prayer of Moses? The one who focuses on one of the two matters, while neglecting the other, falls into error. For Joshua alone could not have won, no matter how fiercely he fought, without the prayer of Moses—that is, without the help of God. And Moses' prayer alone did not mean at all to encourage the army to slack off before the enemy, relying on the prayer of Moses. Struggle and prayer together were proceeding side by side. This [man] struggles in the war, and that [man] lifts up his hands in prayer. The two are inseparable.

The Fellowship [or Communion] of the Holy Spirit

There is a beautiful phrase; if we understand it, we understand a great deal about grace and struggle. The apostolic blessing says, "The grace of the Lord Jesus Christ, and the love of God, and the communion of the Holy Spirit."[247] So what is the meaning of the phrase "the communion of the Holy Spirit"? It is a fellowship between two working together: the Holy Spirit and the person. For the Holy Spirit is able to save and deliver you, but He does not wish to do this alone; rather, He wants you to partner with Him in managing your life—and this is the communion of the Holy Spirit.

Perhaps you might protest and say, "How is that? Can't the

---

246 See Exodus 17:11.
247 2 Corinthians 13:14.

Holy Spirit alone save me?" Yes, He can, but He does not wish to, because it is not in God's policy to force you to do good. For it is not permissible at all that you be rewarded for the work that you have no will in. If the Holy Spirit were the One who worked alone, then why would there be righteous and evil [people]? If the matter were summarized in the work of the Holy Spirit alone, there would not be found a single sinner upon the earth. The Holy Spirit is able to make the sinner repent, but He does not wish to do this unless the will of this sinner is united with Him—it is a fellowship.

The mere existence of a single sinner in the world, who does not repent, is a certain proof that grace alone does not do everything.

Does the Work of Grace Mean the Annulment of Personal Freedom?

No, your freedom remains in force, and so does your will. You can respond to the work of the Holy Spirit in you, to partner with Him, and to obey Him. You can also stop the work of the Holy Spirit in you if you want. Therefore, the Holy Scriptures warn us, saying, "Do not quench the Spirit,"[248] and saying, "Do not grieve the Holy Spirit of God."[249]

Grace is standing at the door, knocking: "Behold, I stand at the door and knock. If anyone hears My voice and opens the door, I will come in to him and dine with him, and he with Me."[250] If he does not open, he is free [to do so], determining his fate as he wills. Grace offers its help to you, and you are free to accept or deny, to work or not.

If you partnered with the Holy Spirit in the work, for the sake of your soul, you would arrive, through the grace of the Holy Spirit, at the perfection of holiness, according to the degree of your response and your obedience [or submission]. If you refuse to partner, then grace does not at all wish to force you to [doing] what is good.

---

248 1 Thessalonians 5:19.
249 Ephesians 4:30.
250 Revelation 3:20.

Many people go into extremes, to the point that the phrase "the personal struggle" seems as though it were a heresy, as though it were a work against the faith and against the help of God! And this is all wrong. Grace is a weapon you are given, with which you can wage war and triumph if you will; you can also neglect it and face the enemy, unarmed, and so you are defeated. In both matters, you are free, doing your will, and it is to your benefit that you use the weapon you are given for the salvation of your soul.

As an example of this matter, we say the following. During a war, if soldiers took from their command tanks, artillery, bombs, and weapons, and they fought and won, would the victory be attributed to their valor or to the weapons? Their valor, without the weapons, would not have been at all sufficient for victory, for a war needs a weapon. Weapons alone, without skilled soldiers to use them, can do nothing on their own. Likewise is the matter in spiritual warfare: it is a partnership between the will of a person and the weapons of the Spirit.

The Necessity of Struggle

Many are the Holy Scriptures that explain the necessity of struggle. Of them, we mention the saying of the Apostle, "Therefore we also, since we are surrounded by so great a cloud of witnesses, let us lay aside every weight, and the sin which so easily ensnares us, and let us run with endurance the race[251] that is set before us."[252] The Apostle says this, and then he rebukes the Hebrews, saying, "You have not yet resisted to bloodshed, striving against sin."[253]

It is necessary, then, that we strive, and not an ordinary striving, but striving to bloodshed against sin. And if someone asks, "Until when is this striving?" we say that it is the striving [or struggle] of the whole life. As the Scripture says, "He who endures to the end will be saved."[254] And the Apostle of the struggle himself explained

---

251 The Arabic word also means "in the struggle."
252 Hebrews 12:1.
253 Hebrews 12:4.
254 Matthew 10:22.

to us how he lived by grace, saying, "I have fought[255] the good fight, I have finished the race, I have kept the faith. Finally, there is laid up for me the crown of righteousness, which the Lord, the righteous Judge, will give to me on that Day."[256]

It is a struggle, but it is not a personal struggle that is separate from the work of God in him. He, however, combines both together, for he says about his preaching, "To this end I also labor, striving according to His working which works in me mightily."[257]

Not of Him Who Wills, Nor of Him Who Runs

As for those who go into extremes in speaking about grace, so that they despise the work of struggle, they protest with the verse that says, "It is not of him who wills, nor of him who runs, but of God who shows mercy."[258] What does this mean? Does this mean that the mercy of God gives us free salvation and conveys us into the kingdom, without running [or pursuing] and without good will? Does this mean that every person sleeps and loiters, not pursuing what is good, nor willing it, content that God would have mercy on him while he is slothful?

It is impossible that the Apostle means this. It is impossible that he means this from his saying "nor of him who runs," while he says, "I have fought the good fight, I have finished the race." He who said "nor of him who runs" has finished the race[259] and received the crown of righteousness as a result of this running [or pursuit] and as a result of this good fight.

He who said "nor of him who runs" is the one who said about himself, "Not that I have already attained, or am already perfected; but I press on,[260] that I may lay hold of that for which Christ Jesus

---

255 The Arabic word is the same as "strive" and "struggle."

256 2 Timothy 4:7–8.

257 Colossians 1:29.

258 Romans 9:16.

259 The words "race" and "runs" are the same word in Arabic, one a noun and the second a verb.

260 The words "press on" and "runs" in the previous verse are the same word in Arabic.

has also laid hold of me. Brethren, I do not count myself to have apprehended; but one thing I do, forgetting those things which are behind and reaching forward to those things which are ahead, I press[261] toward the goal for the prize of the upward call of God in Christ Jesus."[262]

St. Paul himself presses on, that he may lay hold. So, is this just a special test that you only have passed through, Paul? Not at all, it is for all. Therefore, the Apostle continues his word, saying, "Therefore let us, as many as are mature, have this mind."[263] If you are mature, then, you must press on, that you may lay hold. St. Paul the Apostle himself invites all of us to this running [or pursuit] and this struggle, saying, "Do you not know that those who run in a race all run, but one receives the prize? Run in such a way that you may obtain it."[264]

What are you asking of us, O great Apostle? How do we run if the matter "is not of him who wills, nor of him who runs"? What benefit is there from our running and our struggle? It is sufficient for us to sit as we are, and grace comes to us from God, so it conveys us from death to life, and brings us into the kingdom freely, without our willing or running! St. Paul completes his word by saying, "And everyone who competes[265] for the prize is temperate in all things.... Therefore I run thus.... But I discipline my body and bring it into subjection, lest, when I have preached to others, I myself should become disqualified."[266]

Thus, this running and this pressing on are not only for us, the weak believers, but they are also for the Apostles. For St. Paul himself is running, St. Paul who is full of the Holy Spirit, in whom grace worked more than all; he is also in need of running, and of pressing on, and of finishing the race, and of fighting the good fight. And he invites us with him, that we may run like him, that

---

261 Ibid.
262 Philippians 3:12–14.
263 Philippians 3:15.
264 1 Corinthians 9:24.
265 Arabic word is the same as "strives" or "struggles."
266 1 Corinthians 9:25–27.

we may lay hold. What is even more is that we see the great St. Paul disciplining his body and bringing it into subjection, so that he himself may not become disqualified! If St. Paul the Apostle struggles and is afraid of being disqualified, what should we ourselves do?

What is the meaning then of his saying, "It is not of him who wills, nor of him who runs, but of God who shows mercy"?[267] It means that the kingdom does not reach you by only your will or only your running, without the work of God with you, and without the help of His grace, and without the fellowship of the Holy Spirit.

Therefore, the fundamental aspect of this subject is ascribed to God who shows mercy. So, the one who depends on only his will and only his running, is mistaken. For I run, and God shows mercy. When God blesses my running, I ascribe the favor to God, and not to this running. It is true that it is not of him who wills, nor of him who runs, but of God who shows mercy. But who is the one to whom God shows mercy? One of the saints says, "God shows mercy to the ones who will and who run."

This verse reminds me of a saying by St. Paul the Apostle also, "So then neither he who plants is anything, nor he who waters, but God who gives the increase."[268] It is true that the favor is God's, who gives the increase, but God gives the increase to the plant that was planted and watered. The verse does not mean that we do not plant nor water, saying to ourselves, "Neither he who plants is anything, nor he who waters," and afterward we foolishly wait for God to give the increase! Rather, we plant and water, and say, "Neither he who plants is anything, nor he who waters, but God who gives the increase." This is exactly like [the following]: we will and run, and say, "It is not of him who wills, nor of him who runs, but of God who shows mercy."

---

267 Romans 9:16.
268 1 Corinthians 3:7.

Spiritual Warfare

Let us consider the Apostle's explanation of this spiritual warfare in his epistle to the Ephesians:

> Finally, my brethren, be strong in the Lord and in the power of His might. Put on the whole armor of God, that you may be able to stand against the wiles of the devil. For we do not wrestle against flesh and blood, but against principalities, against powers, against the rulers of the darkness of this age, against spiritual hosts of wickedness in the heavenly places. Therefore take up the whole armor of God, that you may be able to withstand in the evil day, and having done all, to stand. Stand therefore, having girded your waist with truth, having put on the breastplate of righteousness, and having shod your feet with the preparation of the gospel of peace; above all, taking the shield of faith with which you will be able to quench all the fiery darts of the wicked one. And take the helmet of salvation, and the sword of the Spirit, which is the word of God; praying always with all prayer and supplication in the Spirit, being watchful to this end with all perseverance and supplication.[269]

Here is a battle. Here is a spiritual warfare and struggle. And the armor is the whole armor of God. This does not mean, however, that we do not struggle. Rather, you must struggle and depend on God in your struggle. Do not be like someone who was given the spiritual weapons of God, and he stood silently without using them and without fighting with them. The weapons are available, but you must fight. The weapons of God are powerful, but unless you use them, you will be defeated. The people whom Paul the Apostle mentioned, weeping, in the epistle to the Philippians,[270] were able to use all these weapons, but they abandoned them. And their souls were inclined toward sin, and they surrendered to it, so they perished in their sins.

---

269 Ephesians 6:10–18.
270 See Philippians 3.

Concerning these spiritual weapons, we note righteousness, truth, the word of God, prayer and supplication, being watchful, and so on. And all these are works. Our teacher Peter the Apostle also speaks about this spiritual warfare, saying, "Be sober, be vigilant; because your adversary the devil walks about like a roaring lion, seeking whom he may devour. Resist him, steadfast in the faith."[271] Our adversary, the devil, is like a roaring lion; what do we do then? "Resist him," that is, struggle, hold your ground, and be valiant, but do not rely on your human arm; rather, "resist him, steadfast in the faith." This verse indicates two matters together: the struggle to resist the devil and the grace on which the struggler relies in the faith.

Paul the Apostle called for such a struggle when he rebuked the Hebrews, saying, "You have not yet resisted to bloodshed, striving against sin."[272] Here is striving, and here is resistance. We do not, however, resist with our own power, but with the whole armor of God, steadfast in the faith. And so did St. Paul the Apostle say to his disciple Timothy, "Fight the good fight of faith."[273] For here is fighting, and here is faith; the two matters go hand in hand together. St. Paul the Apostle spoke about his own struggle, saying, "We were bold in our God to speak to you the gospel of God in much conflict[274]."[275] And he says in the epistle to the Colossians, "For I want you to know what a great conflict I have for you."[276]

The Example of David and Goliath

How was David victorious over Goliath? Was he victorious over him through the grace of God and His help? Yes, undoubtedly. David relied completely on the Lord. Therefore, David said to Goliath, "You come to me with a sword, with a spear, and with a javelin. But I come to you in the name of the LORD of hosts.... This

---

271   1 Peter 5:8–9.
272   Hebrews 12:4.
273   1 Timothy 6:12.
274   Arabic word is the same as "striving" and "struggle."
275   1 Thessalonians 2:2.
276   Colossians 2:1.

day the LORD will deliver you into my hand, and I will strike you and take your head from you.... Then all this assembly shall know that the LORD does not save with sword and spear; for the battle is the LORD's, and He will give you into our hands."[277]

The greatness of David in this war was that he brought God into the battleground. Before the coming of David, there was no talk there about God. There was only talking about this man who had come up, the mighty man who defied the army without care. There was also talk about the king's reward to the one who kills this man.[278]

David, however, brought in the name of the Lord into the battleground: "The LORD, who delivered me from the paw of the lion.... I come to you in the name of the LORD.... The LORD will deliver you into my hand.... the battle is the LORD's," and so on. Was David content by bringing in the name of the Lord into the battleground, saying, "By faith I will kill Goliath, without work nor striving, because the battle is the Lord's, and He will give him into our hands"? No, rather David "chose for himself five smooth stones from the brook, and put them in a shepherd's bag, in a pouch which he had, and his sling was in his hand."[279] And when Goliath drew near to meet David, "that David hurried and ran toward the army to meet the Philistine. Then David put his hand in his bag and took out a stone; and he slung it and struck the Philistine in his forehead, so that the stone sank into his forehead, and he fell on his face to the earth. So David prevailed over the Philistine with a sling and a stone, and struck the Philistine and killed him."—and he was not content by this—"But there was no sword in the hand of David. Therefore David ran and stood over the Philistine, took his sword and drew it out of its sheath and killed him, and cut off his head with it."[280]

It is true that the battle is the Lord's and that the Lord is the one who delivered Goliath into David's hand, but it was necessary

---

277 1 Samuel 17:45–47.

278 See 1 Samuel 17:25.

279 1 Samuel 17:40.

280 1 Samuel 17:48–51.

for David to fight: to hurry and run toward the army, to choose particular stones, to put a stone in the sling, and to skillfully aim. It was also necessary that he draw the sword out, overcome the man, and kill him. All these were works.

In spite of all that, we ascribe the favor to God in this victory, and not to David, because it was possible for the stone not to have hit a deadly spot with respect to Goliath, and so he would not have died. Although David fought with all skillfulness and won, we repeat the saying of Paul the Apostle, "It is not of him who wills, nor of him who runs, but of God who shows mercy."[281] Struggling and works are necessary, and with struggle and work, we ascribe the victory to God.

Faith and Work Together

Likewise, also in the spiritual struggle—it is a war, undoubtedly. You fight with all your strength, and the strength that you have is from God. Do not say, "I sleep and swim in my dreams, and in my dreams, I see that God saves me by His grace!" God does not save the lazy, and grace is not an encouragement to slackness and negligence.

For example, a student does not study but goes to a priest and asks for his prayer in order to succeed, having faith in the power of prayer. What is the judgment on this example? Faith without works is dead. The student must study, and he must also ask for prayer. And so, faith and work are united together.

Some say that struggling [or striving] is a human arm: "Cursed is he who relies on a human arm." The truth is that struggling turns into [reliance on] a human arm if the person relies on themselves *only*; that is, if the person considers that by their struggle only they are saved, without the work of grace with them. Here, the saying of the Master Lord stands before them, "For without Me you can do nothing."[282]

---

281 Romans 9:16.
282 John 15:5.

War, without a weapon, is no good. And a weapon alone, without war and without a person to use it well, cannot bring about victory. The two are inseparable. St. Paul the Apostle had said: "If anyone competes in athletics, he is not crowned unless he competes according to the rules."[283] You must struggle, and struggle according to the rules, and through this, you are saved.

The Struggle of the Apostles and Shepherds

Did the apostles not struggle, and did they not labor for the sake of the faith? St. Paul the Apostle himself says, "I labored more abundantly than they all."[284] They all labored, but Paul labored more, a labor he recorded in his second epistle to the Corinthians.[285] If the matter were grace only, why then would St. Paul labor? What is the point of giving sermons, preaching, counseling, evangelism, guidance, and laboring, so long as grace does everything?

Why does the shepherd labor, guide, visit, and struggle? Is not God able to speak in the hearts of the people, and save them alone? What is the point, then, of the apostles, shepherds, and preachers? What is the point of all the struggle? Do we call all this a human arm? If grace alone does everything, then the priest sleeps and prays in his heart, saying, "You, Lord, take upon Yourself shepherding Your people. Who am I, that I may struggle and guide? It is not of him who wills, nor of him who runs, but You are He who guides the people."

And the preacher, why does he preach? It is sufficient for him to sleep at home, relaxed, saying, "Your grace, Lord, is the one speaking in the hearts of the people, and guiding them, and saving them." And you, why do you weary yourself in your personal life, in prayer, in fasting, in struggling? Relax, relying on [the fact] that grace does everything!

---

283 2 Timothy 2:5.
284 1 Corinthians 15:10.
285 See 2 Corinthians 11:23–33.

Working with God

We say this because many people caused others to be lost by erroneous advice, in which they said, "Do not struggle. Why struggle? God does not begin working with you until you yourself stop [working]; therefore, cancel out your work so that God may work!"

What is this strange, deadly teaching? What is the meaning of "cancel out your work so that God may work"? Why do you not participate in the work with God, so God will work with you, and God will work in you, and God will work through you? As St. Paul said about himself and Apollos, "For we are God's fellow workers."[286] Why do we separate our work from God's work? Why do we not work together, participating with Him, and He with us? So does John the Apostle say about the Lord and the "fellowship with Him."[287] St. Paul the Apostle also speaks about the fellowship of the Holy Spirit.

God, through His grace, through His power, through His Holy Spirit, says to you, "I desire to work with you, to save you. If you consent to working with Me, you are saved, but if you do not consent, you deprive yourself of this salvation. I stand at the door, offering My grace, My love, My power, My help, and all the abilities necessary for the salvation of the soul on whose door I knock. However, if someone opens the door to Me, if he consents to work with Me, if someone delivers himself to Me so that I may work in him, if someone surrenders to My work—then I participate with him, and he with Me."

An Example of Extremism

One of the worst things I have read in my life, regarding extremism in denying the value of works, is what F.B. Meyer wrote in his book *Saved and Kept*. The Protestants who are most fanatic in their war against the struggle [or striving] say that a person has one struggle in their life, that is, the struggle of prayer. This F.B. Meyer, however, wars also against the struggle in prayer. So he says under the title

---

286 1 Corinthians 3:9.
287 1 John 1:6.

"When I had Ceased from my Struggles":

> There is nothing else for you but to come to this. As long as you wrestle with God you miss His richest blessings.... Jacob wrestled with God the whole night and was no further advanced. It was when he could wrestle no more, because the sinew of his strength was shriveled, and he was near falling, and clung to the angel helpless and exhausted, that he received the blessing which made him a prince for the remainder of his days.[288]

Meyer continues and says, "You have agonized and wrestled and entreated, but all has been in vain. Now to quiet. Your gigantic struggles have been drawing the knots tighter."[289] This Protestant book continues to war against prayer, and struggle, and entreating, and wrestling with God, until it says, "Know that God can save you. He has been waiting all this while to save you, and as soon as you come to an end of yourself He will begin."[290] And thus he calls for ceasing[291] from pursuing, saying in another chapter titled "Not 'Attain,' but 'Obtain'":

> You will never get the blessedness for which you long by struggling and agonizing, by your vehement cries and prayers, by your determined resolutions and endeavors; but by stilling yourself before God, and quietly appropriating the abundance of grace.[292]

Then he gave an example of the failure of the struggles of prayer. So he related a story of a person who remained struggling for two years, in which he lifted up prayers to God, that He may give him power to overcome his temptation. And it seemed that the prayers were not heard. And when he was in deep despair, and

288 Meyer F.B., *Saved and Kept*. (Ney York, NY: Fleming H. Revell Company, 1897) 26.
289 Ibid., 29.
290 Ibid.
291 Literally: annulment.
292 Meyer F.B., *Saved and Kept*. (Ney York, NY: Fleming H. Revell Company, 1897) 40.

when he put an end to prayer, God began to work!

Does this teaching satisfy anyone's conscience? The Holy Scriptures call us, in all its books, to struggle in prayer, to pray without ceasing, to watch and pray; but this is Protestant extremism, denying the value of struggle, even in prayer.

Spiritual Exercises

The Protestants, and their followers, of those who war against struggle and work, war against spiritual exercises too, as though they were also a reliance on a human arm.

We say that if a person follows spiritual exercises, depending on his own power, he undoubtedly falls into error. It is good that every person trains themselves, yet depending on the power of God, repeating the saying of St. Paul the Apostle, "I can do all things through Christ who strengthens me."[293] Paul the Apostle speaks of his exercises in the Book of Acts, saying, "I myself always strive[294] to have a conscience without offense toward God and men."[295] He also says in his epistle to the Philippians, "In all things I have learned[296] both to be full and to be hungry, both to abound and to suffer need."[297] He had become exercised in all things, and the exercised senses became his.[298]

There is no objection then that the believer use spiritual exercises, but [even] that they pray to God, saying, "Lead[299] me in Your truth and teach me."[300] In all these exercises, however, the person depends on the power of God that helps them. And in every success of theirs, the person ascribes the favor to God, and not to their own courage or their self-control.

---

293 Philippians 4:13.
294 The word in the Arabic verse is the same as "exercise" or "train."
295 Acts 24:16.
296 The word in the Arabic verse is the same as "exercise" or "train."
297 Philippians 4:12.
298 See Hebrews 5:14.
299 The word in the Arabic verse is the same as "exercise" or "train."
300 Psalms 25:5.

CHAPTER FOUR

Confidence and the Assurance
of [Inheriting] the Kingdom

There are two questions that pass through the mind of many:

1. What are the limits of the hope in the mercies of God?

2. Do the believers have a right to consider the kingdom guaranteed for themselves?

What are the Limits of Hope in the Mercies of God?

1. The Trust in God is Unlimited

Someone might ask, "What are the limits of hope in the mercies of God?" In reality, there are no limits to this hope. This hope in the mercies of God is to the same extent as the measure of them. And so long as the mercies of God are limitless, then also the hope in the mercies of God is limitless.

Hope is one of the three great virtues,[301] and like every virtue, it grows in a person until it reaches its relative perfection in the person. Hope does not reach its perfection unless it is devoid of every doubt and is confirmed with all certainty.

The confidence of hope comes from two matters: one is related to God, and the second to man himself. Hope, with respect to God, is built upon faith in the attributes of God, His prior dealings, the propitiation of His blood, and the truthfulness of His promises.

301 See 1 Corinthians 13:13.

One of the attributes of God is that He is infinite in His mercy, His compassion, His forgiveness, and His love; and that He is not pleased in the death of the sinner, but in that he returns and lives.[302] The prior dealings of God prove to us these attributes. The propitiation of His blood is infinite, sufficient to forgive the sins of the whole world, from the beginning of the ages to their end. As for His promises, they are numerous and true, opening the doors of hope widely before the repentant.

This is one of the aspects of hope. Whoever looks to eternity through it, is filled with hope. As for the second aspect, it is man himself. So, can the look of a person to himself bring confidence in that he is fully assured of[303] the kingdom?

2. Distrust in Our Own Will

I am not in favor of the spiritual song that says, "I am confident..." It is a Protestant song, without a doubt. Although some of its words are sound and true, as a whole nevertheless, it gives a Protestant teaching that is unsound.

If someone asks you, "Are you confident?" what will you answer? Yes, I am confident in the blood of Christ, infinite confidence, but I have no confidence in myself. I have no confidence in my free will, which may incline toward evil. And after I have begun in the Spirit, [yet] I might finish in the flesh.[304] Therefore, those who lose salvation, they lose it, not because God is unable to save them, but because their free will has deviated, [turning] toward evil. So, does a person lose hope? No, this is the extremism into which Cain fell, the first sinner of the sons of Adam, when he said, "My punishment is greater than I can bear!"[305] Into hopelessness, Judas fell also, going and hanging himself.[306]

---

302 See Ezekiel 18:23.
303 Or: guaranteed.
304 See Galatians 3:3.
305 Genesis 4:13.
306 See Matthew 27:5.

As a person errs if they lose hope, so they also err if they rely on a false hope that is built upon their self-righteousness. They likewise err if, in their reliance on the blood of Christ, they forget their diligence and care, and they do not do that which makes them worthy of the efficacy of the blood of Christ. Those also err who think that they have no connection to sin whatsoever, and that they have been renewed, and they have been sanctified, and they are now in another life in which they cannot sin. This is also a false hope, behind which is concealed a kind of self-righteousness, whether the person possessing it is aware of it or not.

We have confidence in the blood of Christ and have confidence in the sufficiency of His propitiation and His redemption. We, however, confess in ourselves that we are sinners and confess that it is very easy for our sin to cause us to be lost. The one who says, "I am guaranteed the kingdom," is as though saying, "I am guaranteed that I will not sin; and if I do sin, then I am guaranteed that I will offer a true and acceptable repentance!" Or such a person might protest against my words, saying, "No, I will not talk about repentance. Rather, if I do sin, 'we have an Advocate with the Father, Jesus Christ the righteous. And He Himself is the propitiation for our sins.'[307]"

Yes, my brother, He is the propitiation for our sins, but He Himself also said, "Unless you repent you will all likewise perish."[308] Do you think He will intercede for you if you do not repent? No, this is a vain illusion. Therefore, you ought to care about your eternity, and repent. Know that Christ will not intercede for the one who does not repent. Rather He warns them, saying, "Hold fast and repent. Therefore if you will not watch, I will come upon you as a thief, and you will not know what hour I will come upon you."[309]

Be humble, then, my brother, and listen to the saying of St. Paul the Apostle who warns, saying, "Therefore let him who thinks

---

307 1 John 2:1–2.
308 Luke 13:3.
309 Revelation 3:3.

he stands take heed lest he fall."[310] You are not stronger than those who fell, but perhaps you have not yet reached the slightest of their stature before they fell. Look to what St. Paul the Apostle says and carefully consider the characteristics he mentions. For he says, "… for those who were once enlightened, and have tasted the heavenly gift, and have become partakers of the Holy Spirit, and have tasted the good word of God and the powers of the age to come, if they fall away…"[311]

How dreadful! How fearful! Have you, you who are guaranteed the kingdom, reached such lofty degrees as those reached? Have you been enlightened, and become partaker of the Holy Spirit, and tasted the good word of God and the powers of the age to come? Nevertheless, those who had received all these gifts fell. And not only did they fall, but they also perished; for the Apostle says, "For it is impossible… to renew them again to repentance,"[312] and he likens them to the earth that is "rejected and near to being cursed, whose end is to be burned."[313]

3. Are You Saved, or Are You Not Saved?

A young man said to me, "What do I answer, then, if someone asks me, saying, 'Are you saved, or are you not saved?'" First you must realize that the one asking this is not purely Orthodox. He must be Protestant, or at least Protestant in their environment and culture. Because the one who ignores your Baptism and what you have received of holy Mysteries, and sows in your soul doubt about your faith, and *now* invites you to the faith and salvation, as though you were Pagan in your previous life—such a person cannot be Orthodox; for their speech betrays them.

As for the answer to their question, it is as follows: yes, I am saved in Baptism from the Original Sin, the inherited Ancestral Sin. I have received this first salvation by the blood of Christ and

---

310 1 Corinthians 10:12.
311 Hebrews 6:4–6.
312 Ibid.
313 Hebrews 6:8.

the efficacy of His propitiation and His redemption. As for the final salvation, we receive it after we put off this body. We are still at war: "For we do not wrestle against flesh and blood, but ... against spiritual hosts of wickedness."[314] We will receive salvation when we overcome and triumph in this war.

So long as we are in this body, we cannot say that we are victorious and are saved. Therefore, the holy Church does not commemorate the saints on their bodily birthday, nor on the day they joined the Church, but on the day of their repose or martyrdom, following the saying of the Scripture: "Remember those ... whose faith follow, considering the outcome of their conduct."[315] Likewise, in the Commemoration of the Saints in the Divine Liturgy, we commemorate the souls of all the righteous who were perfected in the faith, or whose lives were completed in the faith.

Here we mention the story of the repose of the great saint, Abba Macarius the Great, whose spirit was chased by the demons after it left the body. And they said to him, "You are saved, Macarius." But he did not say to them, "Yes, by the grace of Christ, I am saved," except after entering Paradise.[316]

4. Let Your Answer be From the Faith of the Church

If you are asked a doctrinal question, do not, when answering, rely on your own thinking and your own understanding, for the Scriptures said, "Lean not on your own understanding."[317] You are a child of the Coptic Orthodox Church: answer then with the faith of the Coptic Orthodox Church—her faith as it is shown in the authorized Church books, in the sayings of her Fathers, and in her canons and traditions. We will consider now two important books of the Church: the Divine Liturgy book and the Agpeya. Let us see what they teach us in our subject.

---

314 Ephesians 6:12.
315 Hebrews 13:7.
316 See *Bostan Al-Rohban Al-Mowasah, Al-joz' Al-Awal* [The Expanded Paradise of the Monks, Vol. 1]. (Egypt: St. Macarius Monastery, 2006), 301–302.
317 Proverbs 3:5.

Every day you pray in the Eleventh Hour [of the Agpeya] and say, "If the righteous one is scarcely saved, where shall I, the sinner, appear?... O merciful God, count me with the fellows of the eleventh hour." You also say, "For I wasted my life in pleasures and lusts, and the day has passed by me and vanished." And you say, "Every iniquity I did with prudence and activity, and every sin I committed with eagerness and diligence, and of all torment and judgment I am worthy." Is there any phrase in all these that indicates that you are saved, and you are assured of [inheriting] the kingdom, and the matter is over? Or, are they not prayers [springing] from a broken soul, confessing her sins, confessing that she is worthy of all punishment, seeking mercy from the Lord?

With the same contrition, you stand before God in the Twelfth Hour and say, "Behold, I am about to stand before the just judge terrified and trembling because of my many sins. For a life spent in pleasures deserves condemnation. But repent, O my soul, so long as you dwell on this earth." And you rebuke yourself, saying, "If your wicked deeds and ugly evils were exposed before the just judge, what answer would you give while you are lying on the bed of sins, negligent in disciplining the flesh?" It is the contrition of the tax collector who is standing before God in his humiliation, and not the pride of the Pharisee. We do not stand as righteous [men] who have been renewed and sanctified, and have received salvation and been assured of [inheriting] the kingdom; rather, in every prayer, we confess that we are worthy of condemnation and ask for salvation.

And so, in "Graciously accord, O Lord" prayer, in the Twelfth Hour, each of us entreats, saying, "I asked the Lord and said, 'Have mercy on me; save[318] my soul, for I have sinned against You.' Lord, I have fled unto You, save me, and teach me to do Your will."

We also begin the Sixth Hour Prayer with the saying of the psalm, "Save me, O God, by Your name."[319] And in this Hour, we say, "Tear the handwriting of our sins, O Christ our God, and save us." And so the Church teaches you to entreat the Lord every day,

---

318 According to the Arabic text of the prayer.
319 Psalms 54:1.

so that He may tear the handwriting of your sins, and you conclude this litany by saying, "I say my words, and He hears my voice and saves my soul in peace."

You received salvation in Baptism from your Original Sin, and your old man died when you died with Christ and were buried with Him. But you still sin every day, nevertheless. But if you say that you do not sin, you deceive yourself, and the truth is not in you.[320] You sin every day, and the wages of sin is death. Then you are exposed to death every day, and you need salvation every day; you daily need the blood of Christ to cleanse you from every sin. Therefore, you continually need to confess your sins, and repent, and partake of the body of the Lord and His blood, who is "given for us for salvation, remission of sins, and eternal life to those who partake of Him,"[321] as the prayers of the Divine Liturgy teach us.

Then it is a salvation that is renewed continually. You seek it every day and receive it in every repentance, in every absolution that the priest prays over your head, and in every time you partake of the body of the Lord and His blood. After this introduction, let us go back to the subject "Confidence and the Assurance of [Inheriting] the Kingdom."

The Bases of Confidence and Its Conditions as St. John the Apostle Explained Them

The Confidence of Paul and His Certainty

Those who speak about the assurance [or guarantee] of the kingdom foremost rely on St. Paul the Apostle's saying, "Therefore, brethren, having boldness[322] to enter the Holiest by the blood of Jesus,"[323] and his saying about himself, "For I know whom I have believed and am persuaded that He is able to keep what I have committed to Him until that Day,"[324] and, "Finally, there is laid up for me the

---

320 See 1 John 1:8.
321 The Divine Liturgy According to St. Basil – The Confession.
322 Or: confidence.
323 Hebrews 10:19.
324 2 Timothy 1:12.

crown of righteousness,"[325] and so on of Holy Scriptures that many rely on, saying that they live in the "certainty of Paul." We will address all these texts, through the Lord's grace, with explanation and commentary in the following pages.

We, however, would like to first understand the basis upon which this confidence is established. Therefore, in the introduction of this subject, we have not found a better explanation than the beautiful explanation presented by our teacher John the Apostle, about the conditions of confidence, its reasons, and its basis. So, what were the bases of which St. John the Apostle spoke?

1. The Restfulness of the Conscience Condition

St. John the Apostle says, "Beloved, if our heart does not condemn us, we have confidence toward God."[326] Here is a condition: if our heart does not condemn us. That is, if our conscience does not condemn us or reproach us on anything; if we do not sin in anything that would make our heart condemn us.

The source of confidence here, then, and the basis upon which it is established, is that our heart be satisfied with respect to our relationship with God, not condemning us on anything. But if it condemned us, consequently, our confidence would be shaken, undoubtedly.

Then confidence comes from the restfulness of the conscience. And how does this restfulness of the conscience come? St. John clarifies this idea, saying, "Beloved, if our heart does not condemn us, we have confidence toward God. And whatever we ask we receive from Him, because we keep His commandments and do those things that are pleasing in His sight."[327]

The source of this confidence is then made clear: that we keep the commandments of God and do those things that are pleasing in His sight. This is the cornerstone of teaching. So long as we keep the commandments of God and do those things pleasing in His

---

325 2 Timothy 4:8.
326 1 John 3:21.
327 1 John 3:21–22.

sight, then our conscience will be at rest, and there will be nothing on which our heart condemns us; and then we will have confidence toward God.

2. The Abiding in Christ Condition

What else does our teacher St. John the Apostle say? He says, "And now, little children, abide in Him, that when He appears, we may have confidence and not be ashamed before Him at His coming. If you know that He is righteous, you know that everyone who practices righteousness is born of Him."[328] Here is another condition for confidence: that we abide in Christ. So if we do not abide in Christ, we will not have confidence and will be ashamed before Him at His coming. This is a clear teaching.

Do you say then, "I am saved; I am confident; I am guaranteed the kingdom," while your conscience is condemning you on a particular conduct, or while you are not abiding in Christ? Then you are in the position of someone who is deceiving themselves, or who is speaking into the air![329]

Do you want to have confidence? Abide in Christ. If you want to know what it means to abide in Him, let us ask the Book and seek its counsel. St. Paul the Apostle says, "Stand fast therefore in the liberty by which Christ has made us free, and do not be entangled again with a yoke of bondage."[330] That is, do not permit any sin to enslave you. What else also is there in the meaning of "abiding"? St. John the Apostle says, clarifying, "Whoever abides in Him does not sin. Whoever sins has neither seen Him nor known Him."[331] Then if you sin, you do not abide in Him. And if you do not abide in Him, then you have no confidence, and then you will be ashamed before Him at His coming.

How easy then it is to say, "I am confident," or to say, "I am guaranteed the kingdom," without assessing what the Scriptures

---

328   1 John 2:28–29.
329   See 1 Corinthians 14:9.
330   Galatians 5:1.
331   1 John 3:6.

say on the explanation of the meaning of this confidence, which requires that you do not sin.

St. John the Apostle confirms this meaning, saying in the same epistle, "Now he who keeps His commandments abides in Him, and He in him."[332] This is the reciprocal abiding, which comes through keeping the commandments. To what extent does a person keep the commandments? The Apostle answers, "He who says he abides in Him ought himself also to walk just as He walked."[333]

Who dares say, after this explicit text, that they abide in the Lord? And if we do not abide [in Him], how then can we have confidence and not be ashamed before Him at His coming? Therefore, instead of the statements "I am confident" and "I am guaranteed," it is good, after all this, that we stand with the contrite tax collector, so that each of us may beat their heart and say, "God, be merciful to me a sinner!"[334]

You can say that you are confident, and you are assured of the kingdom, if you at all times abide in Christ, walking as He walked also; or at least if you at all times keep His commandments, doing always what pleases Him. For the Apostle says, "But he who does the will of God abides forever."[335] And he also says, "If what you heard from the beginning abides in you, you also will abide in the Son and in the Father."[336]

The Lord of glory Himself explains to us the importance of abiding in Him, saying, "If anyone does not abide in Me, he is cast out as a branch and is withered; and they gather them and throw them into the fire, and they are burned."[337] Do you then want to abide in Him as the branch, and for the sap of the vine to circulate in you, so that you may not dry out; and for you not to be thrown into the fire, so that you are burned? [Then] listen to the Lord say,

---

332 1 John 3:24.
333 1 John 2:6.
334 Luke 18:13.
335 1 John 2:17.
336 1 John 2:24.
337 John 15:6.

"He who eats My flesh and drinks My blood abides in Me, and I in him."[338] What else, Lord? He says, "[He] will live forever."[339]

Thus, of the conditions of confidence are restfulness of the conscience and abiding in the Lord, with all the details that these two conditions entail. What is the third condition, then?

3. The Perfect Love Condition

The Apostle said that one of the conditions of confidence is for the person to abide in God. To abide in God, however, the person must abide in love, because God is love. And so did St. John the beloved say, "God is love, and he who abides in love abides in God, and God in him."[340] So if a person abides in the love of God, and his love is perfected, then they will have confidence. Therefore, the Apostle continues his word, saying, "Love has been perfected among us in this: that we may have boldness[341] in the day of judgment."[342]

How do we abide in the love of God? The Lord Himself says, "If you keep My commandments, you will abide in My love, just as I have kept My Father's commandments and abide in His love."[343] Then, to reach this perfect love that brings confidence, we must, undoubtedly, be perfect in keeping the commandments. Naturally, if we reach this confidence as a result of perfect love, then we will not fear but will be at rest. For this reason, the Apostle continues his word, saying, "There is no fear in love; but perfect love casts out fear."[344]

So, have you, brother, reached this perfect love? Do you love the Lord with all your heart, with all your mind, and with all your strength? In your perfect love for God, do you hate the world with all its pleasures, lusts, and glories, and do you hate even yourself?

---

338   John 6:56.
339   John 6:58.
340   1 John 4:16.
341   Arabic verse: confidence.
342   1 John 4:17.
343   John 15:10.
344   1 John 4:18.

If you are so, and continue to be so, then blessed are you. You may have confidence, so long as you abide in this perfect love.

Final Word

Thus, confidence, which our teacher St. John the Apostle explained, has conditions. Of its conditions is that the person should keep the commandments of God and always do those things that please Him, so that one's conscience may be at rest, and their heart may not condemn them on anything. Also of the conditions is abiding in Christ, with all the meaning this phrase entails. And of its conditions is the arrival at perfect love for God, so that love can cast out fear.

If a person reaches these degrees, they will have perfect confidence and will reach the "certainty of Paul," which they sing of, and it is this that we will explain now. Believe me that the understanding of many of those who say that they have confidence and are assured is very superficial, and they have not reached the true understanding of the meaning of this confidence as St. John the Apostle explained it.

Confidence and Certainty in the Epistles of St. Paul the Apostle

1. Paul's Certainty and His Crown

They say that they are confident of salvation, because St. Paul the Apostle had said, "Finally, there is laid up for me the crown of righteousness,"[345] and because he also said, "For I know whom I have believed and am persuaded that He is able to keep what I have committed to Him until that Day."[346]

---

345 2 Timothy 4:8.
346 2 Timothy 1:12.

a. Who Said These Words?

The first thing we must know is the following: who said these statements? St. Paul the Apostle said them, who is undisputedly one of the greatest apostles. It is the Paul who said, "I have been crucified with Christ; it is no longer I who live, but Christ lives in me."[347] It is the Paul who said, "For I am persuaded[348] that neither death nor life, nor angels nor principalities nor powers, nor things present nor things to come, nor height nor depth, nor any other created thing, shall be able to separate us from the love of God which is in Christ Jesus our Lord."[349] These words were said by Paul who "was caught up to the third heaven,"[350] on whom God had compassion because of the abundance of the revelations.[351]

Are you, you who are confident, like St. Paul the Apostle in the sublimity, the spirituality, and the grace he reached? It is absolutely not permitted that you take the state of the saints and attribute it to yourself. If St. Paul was certain, this does not mean that you are so. Then there is another point.

b. When did St. Paul Say These Words?

These statements St. Paul said at the end of his days; therefore, directly before them, he said, "For I am already being poured out as a drink offering, and the time of my departure is at hand."[352] He also said these after he had "fought the good fight, had finished the race, had kept the faith."[353] There is no objection at all, with respect to a righteous, saintly person in his last days, that the Lord grant him confidence and hope, or that He make him see the crown that is awaiting him, as some of the martyrs saw their crowns before their blood was shed for the sake of Christ. Nevertheless, let us meticulously examine these two statements and see what they refer to.

347 Galatians 2:20.
348 Or: certain, assured.
349 Romans 8:38–39.
350 2 Corinthians 12:2.
351 See 2 Corinthians 12:7.
352 2 Timothy 4:6.
353 Cf. 2 Timothy 4:7.

c. "[I] am Persuaded That He is Able"

St. Paul the Apostle says that he is persuaded that God is able to keep what he has committed to Him. What does this statement mean? Undoubtedly, God is able to keep what any person has committed to Him, but what about the person himself? In what direction is his will heading?

God is able, but perhaps you are not willing; God is able to keep what you have committed to Him, but you, by your free will, might cast it into hell. Did He not say, "How often I wanted … but you were not willing!"[354]? God's ability is a matter no one doubts, but God's ability does not annul your free will. With respect to St. Paul the Apostle, his free will was perfectly in agreement with God's ability to keep what he had committed to Him. Are you likewise? After this, let us address the other statement that was said by the Apostle.

d. "Finally, There is Laid up for me the Crown of Righteousness"

St. Paul the Apostle said, "Finally, there is laid up for me the crown of righteousness, which the Lord, the righteous Judge, will give to me on that Day."[355] He said that the crown was "laid up," but did not say that he had received the crown. For the crown is laid up, which the righteous would receive on that Day. How many people had this crown laid up for them, and they lost it? Therefore, the Lord warns the angel of the church in Philadelphia, saying to him, "Hold fast what you have, that no one may take your crown."[356]

e. What [Else] did the Apostle Say in the Same Epistle?

St. Paul the Apostle said these previously mentioned statements in his second epistle to Timothy. In the same epistle, he also said, "This is a faithful saying: For if we died with Him, we shall also live with Him. If we endure, we shall also reign with Him. If we deny

---

354 Matthew 23:37.
355 2 Timothy 4:8.
356 Revelation 3:11.

Him, He also will deny us."[357] His saying "if we" is a proof that the matter of our salvation does not depend on God only, rather also the person has a say in it. If the matter had been the work of God alone, the freedom of the person would have vanished by that. We also note in the statement, "If we deny Him, He also will deny us," a proof that it is possible for a person to lose their salvation.

2. Confidence to Enter the Holiest

Those who speak about the guarantee of the kingdom rely on the saying of St. Paul the Apostle: "Therefore, brethren, having boldness[358] to enter the Holiest by the blood of Jesus, … let us draw near with a true heart in full assurance of faith, having our hearts sprinkled from an evil conscience and our bodies washed with pure water."[359]

This Scripture speaks about the confidence of entrance and the assurance of faith, with fundamental conditions. For the phrase "having our hearts sprinkled from an evil conscience" indicates the necessity of purity and repentance. And the phrase "our bodies washed with pure water" indicates the necessity of Baptism for salvation.

Was St. Paul content with these words and these two conditions only? No, if we read the rest of his words, we will perceive the opposite of what those who are confident claim. The Apostle continues his word, saying, "Let us hold fast the confession of our hope without wavering, for He who promised is faithful. And let us consider one another in order to stir up love and good works."[360] So, what is the point of the importance of love and good works on this subject of confidence? In his words, St. Paul demonstrates that confidence "to enter the Holiest by the blood of Jesus" depends rather on the works and conduct of a person also; otherwise, this confidence is shaken, and it collapses in a dreadful manner.

---

357 2 Timothy 2:11–12.
358 Arabic verse: confidence.
359 Hebrews 10:19, 22.
360 Hebrews 10:23–24.

Therefore, the Apostle continues his word, warning and admonishing, "For if we sin willfully after we have received the knowledge of the truth, there no longer remains a sacrifice for sins, but a certain fearful expectation of judgment, and fiery indignation which will devour the adversaries."[361] Where is the confidence then, with the existence of this fearful expectation of judgment, if we sin? Does not the matter then require utmost caution and care, and walking in fear and contrition, if we desire to draw near the Holies in confidence?

The Apostle, who spoke about this confidence by the blood of Christ, does not at all forget the justice of God. Rather, he continues his word, saying, "For we know Him who said, 'Vengeance is Mine, I will repay,' says the Lord. And again, 'The LORD will judge His people.' It is a fearful thing to fall into the hands of the living God."[362] This reminds us of what we know about the Protestants: the danger of their employing "the single verse." It would have been better for them, in treating this Holy Scripture of the sayings of St. Paul the Apostle, if they had not taken the first verse of the chapter and had been satisfied with it [only], without following the words of the Apostle to their end. I wish that they had done so, and then they would have seen him say on the subject of confidence the following also: "Therefore do not cast away your confidence, which has great reward. For you have need of endurance, so that after you have done the will of God, you may receive the promise."[363] Truly "for He who promised is faithful," but receiving the promise depends on doing the will of God. For if we do not do the will of God, we will undoubtedly not receive the promise, nor will we have confidence.

What is the meaning of this? Does this mean that God goes back on His gifts which are irrevocable?[364] No, the gifts of God are truly irrevocable, but they have conditions. If you do not receive His gifts, it is not *He* who has gone back on His gifts, but it is

---

361 Hebrews 10:26–27.
362 Hebrews 10:30–31.
363 Hebrews 10:35–36.
364 See Romans 11:29.

you who have transgressed the conditions. God is faithful in His promise, but He said to us by the mouth of His apostle Paul, "After you have done the will of God, you may receive the promise."[365] It is clear that doing the will of God takes the whole of one's life. Therefore, the Apostle said, "For you have need of endurance." This means that we endure all our lives in doing what pleases God, so that we may receive His promises.

Thus, it is made manifest from the words of St. Paul the Apostle in this chapter that "boldness[366] to enter the Holiest by the blood of Jesus" requires many matters: it requires a true heart, the life of repentance and purity, bodies washed with the pure water of Baptism; it also requires the stirring up of love and good works, and doing the will of God, and endurance in all these, and caution against committing sin; otherwise, if we sin by our will, we are exposed to the fearful expectation of judgment, and it is a fearful thing to fall into the hands of the living God.

3. Diligence and Endurance, to Keep the Confidence

It is that endurance about which St. Paul the Apostle spoke in his saying, "Therefore do not cast away your confidence, which has great reward. For you have need of endurance, so that after you have done the will of God, you may receive the promise,"[367] and again he speaks about it, saying, "And we desire that each one of you show the same diligence to the full assurance of hope until the end."[368] Then the assurance of hope needs diligence that a person shows until the end. And to what else? The Apostle continues his word, saying, "That you do not become sluggish, but imitate those who through faith and patience inherit the promises."[369] Here we see that St. Paul has added another thing to faith: patience, that is, endurance. He said that through these, we inherit the promises. Did not the Lord say before, "By your

---

365 Hebrews 10:36.
366 Arabic verse: confidence.
367 Hebrews 10:35–36.
368 Hebrews 6:11.
369 Hebrews 6:12.

patience possess your souls"[370]? And He also said, "He who endures to the end shall be saved."[371]

We received salvation through faith in Baptism. But many forces come together against this salvation, to make us lose it: for against it is our weak will that often inclines to evil, and against it is our enemy who "walks about like a roaring lion, seeking whom he may devour,"[372] and against our salvation also is sin which "has cast down many wounded, and all who were slain by her were strong men."[373] In all this, we need to "run with endurance the race that is set before us,"[374] and to remain thus enduring until the end of our life [or conduct]; therefore, the Scripture says, "Considering the outcome of their conduct."[375]

4. He Who has Begun a Work in You Will Complete it

Those who advocate for confidence and assurance of the kingdom depend also on the saying of St. Paul to the Philippians: "Being confident of this very thing, that He who has begun a good work in you will complete it until the day of Jesus Christ."[376] We reiterate what we have previously said, that God is able to complete it in us, but what about our own position? In the foolish Galatians God had begun a good work; nevertheless, St. Paul says to them, "Are you so foolish? Having begun in the Spirit, are you now being made perfect by the flesh?"[377] Here they are the ones who will continue by the flesh, not giving Him an opportunity to complete a good work in them.

As for the Philippians, despite St. Paul the Apostle's confidence, we see him praying for their sakes, that their love may abound, that they may abound in all knowledge, that they "may be sincere and

---

370 Luke 21:19.
371 Matthew 24:13.
372 1 Peter 5:8.
373 Proverbs 7:26.
374 Hebrews 12:1.
375 Hebrews 13:7.
376 Philippians 1:6.
377 Galatians 3:3.

without offense till the day of Christ, being filled with the fruits of righteousness."[378] Although Christ is able to complete, there is, however, work laid upon them themselves: that they may be without offense until the end. He also commanded them, saying, "Let your conduct be worthy of the gospel of Christ."[379] He said to them, "For to you it has been granted on behalf of Christ, not only to believe in Him, but also to suffer for His sake, having the same conflict which you saw in me and now hear is in me."[380]

So, what is the meaning of all this? So long as God would complete what He had begun in them, what is the point of these counsels: that they abound in love and understanding, that they be without offense, that they be filled with the fruits of righteousness, that their conduct be worthy of the gospel of Christ, that they suffer for His sake, that they have the same conflict of St. Paul? This is because, as Christ has a part in their salvation, so they too have a part they must accomplish [i.e., work out]. Therefore, he said to them, "Work out your own salvation with fear and trembling."[381] Christ will not complete the work alone; rather, He will complete it through them, in them, and with them. God does not take people by force and throw them into the kingdom; rather, they must work with Him.

Therefore, we find that the epistle to the Philippians is the epistle in which St. Paul the Apostle says the most that he presses on that he may lay hold.[382] St. Paul has also given[383] an example to them in the same epistle, of those who began yet did not finish well, and so their end was perdition. The Apostle mentioned them, weeping. St. Paul the Apostle asked them to follow his example of pressing on and striving, and not to follow the example of those who are perishing.[384]

---

378 Philippians 1:9–11.
379 Philippians 1:27.
380 Philippians 1:29–30.
381 Philippians 2:12.
382 See Philippians 3:12, 14.
383 Literally: explained.
384 See Philippians 3:17.

Concluding Remark on the Subject of Confidence

How beautiful is the saying of Solomon the wise in this area: "A wise man fears and departs from evil, but a fool rages and is self-confident."[385] Therefore, our teacher St. Paul the Apostle advises us, saying, "Do not be haughty, but fear."[386] And he has advised the Philippians, saying, "Work out your own salvation with fear and trembling."[387] St. Peter the Apostle joins his voice to this advice, saying, "And if you call on the Father, who without partiality judges according to each one's work, conduct yourselves throughout the time of your stay here in fear."[388]

So long as there is confidence, certainty, and guarantee of the kingdom, what is then the meaning of fear and trembling? Why does a person not rely on God's promises and be reassured? Yes, we are reassured with respect to God's promises, but we are not reassured with respect to ourselves. Therefore, the Apostle blended the speech on the divine promises with the speech on fear, saying, "Therefore, having these promises, beloved, let us cleanse ourselves from all filthiness of the flesh and spirit, perfecting holiness in the fear of God."[389]

---

385 Proverbs 14:16.
386 Romans 11:20.
387 Philippians 2:12.
388 1 Peter 1:17.
389 2 Corinthians 7:1.

CHAPTER FIVE

Is it Possible for the
Believer to Perish?

It is Possible for the Believer to Fall

Perhaps of the most famous examples of this are some of the angels of the seven churches in Asia; those were undoubtedly believers. And the stories of their fall we will explain in the coming pages. And how easy it is to state many examples of prophets and saints who fell. We will not, however, linger for long on this point, because most of the Protestant groups, the Salvation of Souls Society, and Plymouth, agree that it is possible for the believer to fall, but they say that the believer cannot perish. Therefore, let this last point be the subject of our research and proof: the possibility that the believer perishes.

The Word "Believer" and the Word "Elect"

All the elect are believers, but not all the believers are elect, for some of them might fall and perish. The error of the Protestants is that whenever we mention to them a story of a believer who had perished, they argue, saying, "No, he was not a believer. If he had been a believer, he would not have perished."[390] We will try in this research to conclusively prove the faith of each example of the examples we are including of those who perished.

---

390 See pages 24–26 in this book for further explanation.

The First Proof

The Example of the Branch That is Cut Off
(Romans 11 and John 15)

After St. Paul the Apostle had likened the Jews to natural branches that were broken off the root and the fatness of the olive tree, he said, "You will say then, 'Branches were broken off that I might be grafted in.' Well said. Because of unbelief they were broken off, and you stand by faith."[391] It is clear here that he is speaking to a believer who was confirmed[392] in the olive tree, was grafted into it, and became "a partaker of the root and fatness of the olive tree."[393] So what does he say to this believer? He says to this believer, "Do not be haughty, but fear. For if God did not spare the natural branches, He may not spare you either. Therefore consider the goodness and severity of God: on those who fell, severity; but toward you, goodness, if you continue in His goodness. Otherwise you also will be cut off."[394] The last phrase—"you also will be cut off"—is a warning to this believer about the possibility of his destruction if he does not continue in God's goodness.

This example resembles what the Lord Christ said when He likened Himself to the vine and likened us to the branches. The branches that are in the vine refer to the believers, undoubtedly. Because the branch is a member of the members of the vine, its sap flows in it. So, is it possible for it to perish? The Master Lord says, "Every branch in Me that does not bear fruit He takes away.... If anyone does not abide in Me, he is cast out as a branch and is withered; and they gather them and throw them into the fire, and they are burned."[395] This means that such an unfruitful believer will inevitably perish.

391　Romans 11:19–20.

392　This word is the same as the Arabic word in Romans 11:20 that appears as "stand" in NKJV.

393　Romans 11:17.

394　Romans 11:20–22.

395　John 15:2, 6.

The Second Proof

The Example of the Disobedient People in the Wilderness
(Hebrews 3 and 4)

In these two chapters, St. Paul the Apostle is speaking to "holy brethren, partakers of the heavenly calling."[396] So, were these holy people [or saints] of the believers, or not? Naturally, they were believers, and there is no doubt. These the Apostle warns against "departing from the living God."[397] And, of course, warning against departing is directed to believers rather than to unbelievers.

To those holy brethren, the believers, partakers of the heavenly calling, the Apostle says, "Therefore, as the Holy Spirit says: 'Today, if you will hear His voice, do not harden your hearts as in the rebellion, in the day of trial in the wilderness.'"[398] What is this day of rebellion? What happened in it? And what does it indicate in this matter of ours? Those who rebelled against the Lord are the disobedient people in the wilderness, with whom the Lord was angry for forty years, and He said, "So I swore in My wrath, 'They shall not enter My rest.'"[399] And so they perished in the wilderness, "whose corpses fell in the wilderness."[400]

Those who fell, of whom God swore that they would not enter His rest, who rebelled against the Lord in the wilderness—did they receive salvation before, or did they not receive it? St. Paul the Apostle answers, saying, "For who, having heard, rebelled? Indeed, was it not all who came out of Egypt, led by Moses?"[401] They received the first salvation: the Lord delivered them from slavery, and split the Red Sea for them, and they passed in the midst of the water, which is a symbol of Baptism, and they crossed the Sea. Despite all this, however, they perished in the wilderness and lost the salvation they had received, and the Lord swore that they would not enter His rest.

---

396 Hebrews 3:1.
397 Hebrews 3:12.
398 Hebrews 3:7–8.
399 Hebrews 3:11.
400 Hebrews 3:17.
401 Hebrews 3:16.

Do not those present a clear example of the believers who perish? Those disobedient undoubtedly represent those who depart from the faith, so they perish. They had perished because of the disobedience, and other people entered the promised land: "Those to whom it was first preached did not enter because of disobedience."[402] Of this disobedience that prevents [a person] from entering the Lord's rest, the Apostle warns us, saying, "Let us therefore be diligent to enter that rest, lest anyone fall according to the same example of disobedience."[403] He even says more than this: "Therefore, since a promise remains of entering His rest, let us fear lest any of you seem to have come short of it."[404]

The story of these disobedient people that had lost their first salvation and perished, is given to us as an example, so that we may learn and realize that it is possible for the believer to lose their salvation. "Now all these things happened to them as examples, and they were written for our admonition, upon whom the ends of the ages have come. Therefore let him who thinks he stands take heed lest he fall."[405] The story of the perdition of this disobedient people reminds us of Lot's wife, who was saved from Sodom yet perished outside it; therefore, the Scripture says, "Remember Lot's wife."[406]

The Third Proof

"If we sin willfully after we have received the knowledge of the truth." (Hebrews 10:29–32).

St. Paul the Apostle speaks with the same "holy brethren, partakers of the heavenly calling,"[407] who after they "were illuminated,

---

402 Hebrews 4:6.
403 Hebrews 4:11.
404 Hebrews 4:1.
405 1 Corinthians 10:11–12.
406 Luke 17:32.
407 Hebrews 3:1.

... endured a great struggle with sufferings,"[408] and who "had compassion on me in my[409] chains, and joyfully accepted the plundering of your goods, knowing that you have a better and an enduring possession for yourselves in heaven."[410] What did he say to those with whom he had begun his speech, saying, "Therefore, brethren, having boldness to enter the Holiest by the blood of Jesus"[411]? He said to them:

> For if we sin willfully after we have received the knowledge of the truth, there no longer remains a sacrifice for sins, but a certain fearful expectation of judgment, and fiery indignation which will devour the adversaries.... For we know Him who said, "Vengeance is Mine, I will repay," says the Lord. And again, "The LORD will judge His people." It is a fearful thing to fall into the hands of the living God.[412]

This is a warning of perdition to whoever sins of those believing, holy brethren, giving us an idea about the possibility of perdition of the believer. On this, St. Paul the Apostle says, "Of how much worse punishment, do you suppose, will he be thought worthy who has trampled the Son of God underfoot, counted the blood of the covenant by which he was sanctified a common thing, and insulted the Spirit of grace?"[413] We note here that the phrase "the blood of the covenant by which he was sanctified" indicates that this person who perished was a believer, who had been sanctified before by the blood of the covenant.

---

408   Hebrews 10:32.
409   I.e., St. Paul's.
410   Hebrews 10:34.
411   Hebrews 10:19.
412   Hebrews 10:26–27, 30–31.
413   Hebrews 10:29.

The Fourth Proof

Examples of Perdition of the Apostate

Those apostates were believers before, then they departed [from the faith] and perished. Examples in the Holy Scriptures are many, illustrating their perdition. St. Paul the Apostle says to his disciple Timothy:

> Now the Spirit expressly says that in latter times some will depart from the faith, giving heed to deceiving spirits and doctrines of demons, speaking lies in hypocrisy, having their own conscience seared with a hot iron, forbidding to marry, and commanding to abstain from foods which God created to be received with thanksgiving by those who believe and know the truth.[414]

Those who gave heed to deceiving spirits and doctrines of demons had undoubtedly perished. Nevertheless, the phrase "some will depart from the faith" indicates that they were believer before. This is a clear example of the possibility of the perdition of the believer if they apostatize, which includes all the heretics.

Also, one of the examples of the apostates is what was mentioned in the parable of the sower. The Lord said, "But the ones on the rock are those who, when they hear, receive the word with joy; and these have no root, who believe for a while and in time of temptation fall away."[415] We cannot believe that there would be salvation for those on the rock, who apostatize in the time of temptation; nevertheless, Christ Himself called them believers though [only] for a while.

Of the gravest kinds of apostasy is the general apostasy that will happen before the Second Coming of Christ. On this, the Apostle said about the Second Coming of Christ, "Let no one deceive you by any means; for that Day will not come unless the falling away comes first, and the man of sin is revealed, the son of perdition, who opposes and exalts himself above all that is called God."[416] In

---

414   1 Timothy 4:1–3.

415   Luke 8:13. The word "fall away" in the Arabic verse is the same as "apostatize."

416   2 Thessalonians 2:3–4.

this general apostasy, many of the believers will undoubtedly perish who fall away from the faith.

And of the examples of the heretics, the corrupt, and those who apostatize and perish, St. Peter the Apostle said about them, "For if, after they have escaped the pollutions of the world through the knowledge of the Lord and Savior Jesus Christ, they are again entangled in them and overcome, the latter end is worse for them than the beginning. For it would have been better for them not to have known the way of righteousness, than having known it, to turn from the holy commandment delivered to them."[417]

The Fifth Proof

Those Who Were Enlightened and Fell (Hebrews 6:4–8)

St. Paul the Apostle says, "For it is impossible for those who were once enlightened, and have tasted the heavenly gift, and have become partakers of the Holy Spirit, and have tasted the good word of God and the powers of the age to come, if they fall away, to renew them again to repentance."[418] The first qualities point to the faith of those, and the last phrase points to their perdition. This is a clear proof of the possibility of the perdition of the believer. But the Protestants, very unfortunately, try to claim that those were not believers, despite that they were enlightened, were partakers of the Holy Spirit, and had tasted the heavenly gift, the good word of God, and the powers!

We do not desire to argue much with them; rather, it is sufficient to say that the wording of the verse points to their faith. For the phrase "it is impossible ... to renew them again to repentance" is a clear evidence that they had been previously renewed, that is, they were believers. And their perdition is clear from the Apostle's likening them to the earth that "is rejected and near to being cursed, whose end is to be burned."[419]

---

417 2 Peter 2:20–21.
418 Hebrews 6:4–6.
419 Hebrews 6:8.

The Sixth Proof
Assurance Requires Steadfastness and has Conditions

St. Peter the Apostle says, "Therefore, brethren, be even more diligent to make your call and election sure, for if you do these things you will never stumble."[420] Thus, God's election of us and His call to us require of us even more diligence, so that this election may be sure; otherwise, the election is not sure.

This also resembles the saying of St. Paul, "Whose [i.e., Christ's] house we are if we hold fast the confidence and the rejoicing of the hope firm to the end."[421] It is as though this confidence may or may not remain firm, and it requires that we hold fast to it to the end. Also, the Apostle continues, saying, "For we have become partakers of Christ if we hold the beginning of our confidence steadfast to the end."[422] Here is a condition that is our duty, that "we hold ... to the end." The Apostle continues his word, warning us against hardening our hearts; otherwise, what happened to the disobedient people who perished in the wilderness would happen to us.

Again, the Apostle repeats this condition that is our duty, in his saying, "To present you holy, and blameless, and above reproach in His sight—if indeed you continue in the faith, grounded and steadfast, and are not moved away from the hope of the gospel."[423] It is salvation from the Lord; we have hope in it. The Apostle, however, warns us, saying, "How shall we escape if we neglect so great a salvation…?"[424] Thus, it is possible for us to neglect the salvation, so we escape not.

---

420 2 Peter 1:10.
421 Hebrews 3:6.
422 Hebrews 3:14.
423 Colossians 1:22–23.
424 Hebrews 2:3.

The Seventh Proof

Revelation 13:7

How grave is the saying about the beast in the Book of Revelation, that "it was granted to him to make war with the saints and to overcome them."[425] The word "saints" means that they were undoubtedly believers. So if it is possible for the saints to be overcome, let us be on our guard, and let us persist in prayer always, that the Lord may have mercy on us, so that we may not perish.

The Eighth Proof

The Perdition of Demas, the Assistant of St. Paul

Demas was one of the assistants of St. Paul the Apostle. He mentioned him in his epistle to the Colossians: "Luke the beloved physician and Demas greet you,"[426] and his epistle to Philemon, he said, "Epaphras, my fellow prisoner in Christ Jesus, greets you, as do Mark, Aristarchus, Demas, Luke, my fellow laborers."[427] Here he mentions him among three of the greatest preachers working with him, two of whom are of the four evangelists. And the name of Demas comes before the name of St. Luke the Evangelist. Was he, nevertheless, not a believer? Demas, the believer, the great preacher, had perished, nevertheless. St. Paul said about him, "Demas has forsaken me, having loved this present world."[428] And the Protestants say in their books that after he had left St. Paul, he became a pagan priest.

The Remaining Proofs

To avoid repetition, see the proofs related to this subject that were stated in the section titled "Judgment According to Works" in the second chapter.

---

425 Revelation 13:7.
426 Colossians 4:14.
427 Philemon 23–24.
428 2 Timothy 4:10.

Protests and the Response to Them

The First Protest

"No one is able to snatch them out of My Father's hand"
(John 10:27–29).

Their first protest on the possibility of the perdition of the believer
is the saying of the Lord:

> My sheep hear My voice, and I know them, and they
> follow Me. And I give them eternal life, and they shall
> never perish; neither shall anyone snatch them out of My
> hand. My Father, who has given them to Me, is greater
> than all; and no one is able to snatch them out of My
> Father's hand.[429]

So, what is the meaning of this Scripture? I wish that we would
consider it well.

1. The first attribute the Lord mentioned about those who do
not perish is that they were sheep. The Lord Christ likened the
righteous to sheep, while He likened the wicked to goats. He also
mentioned that on the day of judgment, "all the nations will be
gathered before Him, and He will separate them one from another,
as a shepherd divides his sheep from the goats. And He will set the
sheep on His right hand, but the goats on the left. Then the King
will say to those on His right hand, 'Come, you blessed of My
Father, inherit the kingdom prepared for you from the foundation
of the world.'"[430] So long as these are sheep, then they are righteous
people, because if they had been wicked, He would have called
them goats.

2. He gave these sheep descriptions of righteousness, of which:

a. He says that they hear My voice and follow Me. This
means that they carry out the commandments and do good

---

429 John 10:27–29.
430 Matthew 25:32–34.

deeds. And we will agree that whoever hears the voice of the Lord and follows Him cannot perish.

b. In the same chapter, He described the sheep as that "they will by no means follow a stranger, but will flee from him, for they do not know the voice of strangers,"[431] and that they do not hear the voice of thieves and robbers who came before Him.[432] All this means that these good sheep do not go after the demons, nor after the wicked.

All this indicates goodness from both of its aspects, the positive and negative: they follow the Lord, but do not follow the stranger. They know the voice of the Lord, distinguish it, hear it, and follow it; but they do not know the voice of strangers and do not follow them; rather, they flee from them. We do not see for goodness more proofs than these; nevertheless, we will mention another proof.

3. He says, "My sheep hear My voice, and I know them." This knowledge is reciprocal; therefore, in the same chapter, He says, "I know My sheep, and am known by My own. As the Father knows Me, even so I know the Father."[433] What knowledge is greater than this! The Lord elaborates on this knowledge, saying that He "calls his own sheep by name."[434] This knowledge distinguishes the good from the evil [people] to whom the Lord says, "I never knew you; depart from Me, you who practice lawlessness!"[435] The Lord, then, said about the evildoers that He did not know them, and this is confirmed also by the saying of the Lord to the foolish virgins: "Assuredly, I say to you, I do not know you."[436] Therefore, so long as He knows these sheep that will not be snatched out of His hand nor the Father's hand, then these must be pure of heart and good, because if they had been evil, He would have said to them, "I do not know you."

---

431 John 10:5.
432 See John 10:8.
433 John 10:14–5.
434 John 10:3.
435 Matthew 7:23.
436 Matthew 25:12.

We then summarize the attributes of these believers who will not be snatched out of the Father's hand, as follows: they are sheep and not goats, that is, they are good and righteous; also they obey the commandments of God, so they hear His voice and follow Him; likewise, they stay away from evil and evildoers, not hearing the voice of a stranger nor follow him, rather they flee from him. We, without a doubt, agree that [people] of this kind do not perish.

4. What is understood from the statement "No one is able to snatch them out of My Father's hand"? It means that the external powers are not able to snatch them out of the Father's hand; this, however, does not prevent the believer, while in the Father's hand, having perfect freedom, from falling by their own will. God does not permit an external power to triumph over you while you are in His hand; your internal will, however, can cause you to perish if you will. If you say to Him, "Lord, help my weakness," He will drive away all the opposing powers from you. But if, by yourself, you want to abandon Him, He will not force you to remain with Him.

What is your opinion on some sheep that were in Christ's hand, but went astray, fell, and needed repentance, about some of which it was said that they had a name that they were alive but were dead?[437] Such examples are some of the seven angels who were mentioned in the Book of Revelation. St. John of Revelation said that he saw the Lord Christ in the midst of seven lampstands, which are the seven churches. "He had in His right hand seven stars.... The seven stars are the angels of the seven churches."[438] And the Lord began the first letter by saying, "These things says He who holds the seven stars in His right hand."[439] Then, not only are they in His hand, but also in His *right* hand, and the word "right" denotes power: "The right hand of the Lord has wrought mightily. The right hand of the Lord has exalted me."[440]

Those who are in the Lord's right hand, those mighty shepherds

---

437 See Revelation 3:1.
438 Revelation 1:16, 20.
439 Revelation 2:1.
440 Psalms 117:15–16 LXX.

of the churches—what did the Lord say to them? He said terrifying words to them. He said to the angel of the church in Ephesus, "Remember therefore from where you have fallen; repent and do the first works, or else I will come to you quickly and remove your lampstand from its place."[441] How dreadful!

He said to the angel of the church in Sardis, "I know your works, that you have a name that you are alive, but you are dead."[442] Imagine this great angel, whom the Lord was holding in His right hand, was dead and needed the Lord to say to him, "Remember therefore how you have received and heard; hold fast and repent. Therefore if you will not watch, I will come upon you as a thief, and you will not know what hour I will come upon you."[443] May God have mercy on us, my brethren, according to His great mercy. We are not stronger than these seven angels.

Hear also the terrifying words that the Lord said to the angel of the church in Laodicea: "So then, because you are lukewarm, and neither cold nor hot, I will vomit you out of My mouth."[444] It is a threat of perdition. The Lord continues His word, saying to him, "Because you say, I am rich, have become wealthy, and have need of nothing'—and do not know that you are wretched, miserable, poor, blind, and naked."[445] Therefore, the Lord counselled him to buy "white garments, that you may be clothed, that the shame of your nakedness may not be revealed."[446] Finally, He said to him, "Be zealous and repent."[447]

Therefore, brother, do not depend on that you are in the hand of God, and abandon your first love. For how easy it is for you to fall from the right hand of God if *you* want [or will] that. No one snatches you from His hand, but rather you, by your own will, might leave the hand of God.

---

441 Revelation 2:5.
442 Revelation 3:1.
443 Revelation 3:3.
444 Revelation 3:16.
445 Revelation 3:17.
446 Revelation 3:18.
447 Revelation 3:19.

The Second Protest

"You were sealed with the Holy Spirit of promise"
(Ephesians 1:13–14).

Another verse on which the protesters depend is the saying of St. Paul the Apostle, "Having believed, you were sealed with the Holy Spirit of promise, who is the guarantee of our inheritance."[448] They consider the seal of the Holy Spirit as a guarantee of eternal inheritance that is not taken away from the person.

The response is simple: those who were sealed with the Holy Spirit still have free will; therefore, the Scripture says, "Do not grieve the Holy Spirit of God, by whom you were sealed for the day of redemption,"[449] and says to them also, "Do not quench the Spirit,"[450] and says more than this, "He who blasphemes against the Holy Spirit never has forgiveness, but is subject to eternal condemnation."[451] Then the matter is still in the hand of man, who is free to do as he wills. If he wishes, he grieves the Spirit; and if he wishes, he quenches the Spirit; and if he wishes, he blasphemes against the Spirit. Therefore, we pray and say with the psalmist, "Do not take Your Holy Spirit from me."[452]

King Saul, whom the Lord chose, whom Samuel anointed with the holy oil, on whom the Holy Spirit came and so he prophesied, and he was turned into another man,[453] to the extent that the people marveled, saying, "Is Saul also among the prophets?"[454]— the Lord went back and rejected this Saul, and the Spirit of the Lord departed from him, and a distressing spirit from the Lord troubled him,[455] and Saul perished, being rejected by God. The moral is not in the beginnings of the person, having been sealed with the Holy Spirit or having the Spirit of the Lord come upon

---

448 Ephesians 1:13–14.
449 Ephesians 4:30.
450 1 Thessalonians 5:19.
451 Mark 3:29.
452 Psalms 51:11.
453 See 1 Samuel 10:6–11.
454 1 Samuel 10:11.
455 See 1 Samuel 16:1, 14.

them, but rather the moral is how their end is.

With this same response, we also answer those who protest with the saying of the Lord, "And I will pray the Father, and He will give you another Helper, that He may abide with you forever."[456] The Spirit is ready to abide with us; if we continue, however, in grieving the Spirit and quenching the Spirit, or in finally blaspheming against the Spirit, then it is possible that He be taken away from us.

The Third Protest

"Your names are written in heaven"
(Luke 10:20; Philippians 4:3; Revelation 21:27)

Some protest against the possibility of the believer's perdition, by the saying of the Lord to the seventy disciples: "Nevertheless do not rejoice in this, that the spirits are subject to you, but rather rejoice because your names are written in heaven,"[457] and by the saying of St. Paul the Apostle in his epistle to the Philippians, "And the rest of my fellow workers, whose names are in the Book of Life," or by the saying of the divine inspiration in the Book of Revelation, "There shall by no means enter it anything that defiles, or causes an abomination or a lie, but only those who are written in the Lamb's Book of Life."[458] How easy it is to say that the elect are meant by these Holy Scriptures, especially the last Scripture. More evident than this, however, is that we say in utter honesty that it is possible for a person's name to be written in the Book of Life, and then their name be erased afterward. This is clear from the words of the Lord to Moses the prophet in the Book of Exodus, when Moses said to Him, "'Yet now, if You will forgive their sin—but if not, I pray, blot me out of Your book which You have written.' And the LORD said to Moses, 'Whoever has sinned against Me, I will blot him out of My book.'"[459]

---

456 John 14:16.
457 Luke 10:20.
458 Revelation 21:27.
459 Exodus 32:32–33.

In the Book of Revelation, the Lord said, "He who overcomes shall be clothed in white garments, and I will not blot out his name from the Book of Life."[460] Then there is a possibility for a person's name to be blotted out from the Book of Life: whoever overcomes, the Lord will not blot out their name, and whoever is overcome, it is possible for the Lord to blot out their name from the Book of Life. He also said, "Whoever has sinned against Me, I will blot him out of My book." He also said at the end of the Book of Revelation, "If anyone takes away from the words of the book of this prophecy, God shall take away his part from the Book of Life, from the holy city, and from the things which are written in this book."[461]

⌒

The Fourth Protest

We are Sons of God and Heirs with Christ
(Galatians 4:7)

They also protest with the saying of St. Paul the Apostle, "Therefore you are no longer a slave but a son, and if a son, then an heir of God through Christ."[462] This protest calls us to research together what the spiritual meaning of the word "son" is. On the definition of the word "son," St. John the Apostle says, "If you know that He is righteous, you know that everyone who practices righteousness is born of Him."[463] If you, brother, said that you are a son of God, and consequently an heir of God through Christ, then you must prove your sonship through your righteousness. If you do not practice righteousness, you are not born of Him.

St. John also says, "Whoever has been born of God does not sin, for His seed remains in him; and he cannot sin, because he has been born of God. In this the children of God and the children of the devil are manifest: Whoever does not practice righteousness

---

460 Revelation 3:5.
461 Revelation 22:19.
462 Galatians 4:7.
463 1 John 2:29.

is not of God."[464] Our teacher St. John the beloved repeats this understanding in the fifth chapter of his epistle, saying, "We know that whoever is born of God does not sin; but he who has been born of God keeps himself, and the wicked one does not touch him."[465]

So, are you a son with this meaning, which St. John the Apostle explained? If you are so, then blessed are you; undoubtedly, you are an heir of God through Christ. However, when someone discusses with you a verse related to the subject of salvation, if you fight, and revile, and raise your voice, and make a fuss, and then say that you are s son of God, know that the sons of God do not revile, because revilers do not inherit the kingdom of God.[466] Do not boast vainly, brother, as the Jews in the past boasted about their sonship to Abraham. So the Lord Christ embarrassed them, saying, "If you were Abraham's children, you would do the works of Abraham."[467] If you were a son of God and an heir with Christ, "you ought yourself also to walk just as He walked."[468]

Being born of God is not a mere sham title in which we boast; it rather has distinguishing marks. The Apostle says, "For whatever is born of God overcomes the world,"[469] and says, "Everyone who loves is born of God and knows God."[470] Do these two conditions apply to you? Do you abide in love? And do you overcome the world?

Another essential mark for being born of God is made manifest in the saying of St. Paul the Apostle to the Romans: "For if you live according to the flesh you will die; but if by the Spirit you put to death the deeds of the body, you will live. For as many as are led by the Spirit of God, these are sons of God."[471] Here is a condition for

---

464 1 John 3:9–10.

465 1 John 5:18.

466 See 1 Corinthians 6:10.

467 John 8:39.

468 Cf. 1 John 2:6.

469 1 John 5:4.

470 1 John 4:7.

471 Romans 8:13–14.

the sonship to God, which the Apostle specifies: being led by the Spirit. Who is a son of God? It is he who is led by the Spirit. Does this condition apply to you, O you who are an heir with Christ and are guaranteed the kingdom? Ask yourself.

Yet another fundamental condition for being a son of God is that you be born from above, be born of water and the Spirit. This is because our Lord Jesus Christ Himself said to Nicodemus, "Most assuredly, I say to you, unless one is born of water and the Spirit, he cannot enter the kingdom of God."[472] So, have you also been saved "through the washing of regeneration and renewing of the Holy Spirit"[473]? And has the Lord Christ sanctified you, cleansing you with the washing of water by the word?[474]

Do not say, without careful consideration, "I am a son of God, so I am an heir of Christ, guaranteed the kingdom." Rather, examine yourself. Have you been born of water and the Spirit? Do you keep yourself, and the wicked one does not touch you? Do you overcome the world? Do you love and practice righteousness? Are you unable to sin? Are you led by the Spirit of God? If you were so, then you would truly be a son of God, and your works would reveal you: "You will know them by their fruits."[475]

As for St. Paul's saying, "You are no longer a slave but a son,"[476] we must place next to it the saying of the Lord Christ: "Whoever commits sin is a slave of sin. And a slave does not abide in the house forever, but a son abides forever. Therefore if the Son makes you free, you shall be free indeed."[477] Then of the marks of the sonship to God is freedom from sin and not being a slave of it. If you still commit sin, then you are a slave of it, and consequently, you are excluded from the saying of St. Paul the Apostle: "You are no longer a slave but a son."

The Lord Christ settles this matter, saying, "Not everyone who

---

472 John 3:5.
473 Titus 3:5.
474 See Ephesians 5:26.
475 Matthew 7:16.
476 Galatians 4:7.
477 John 8:34–36.

says to Me, 'Lord, Lord,' shall enter the kingdom of heaven, but he who does the will of My Father in heaven,"[478] "for whoever does the will of My Father in heaven is My brother and sister and mother."[479] This truly is the heir with Christ. The same aforesaid words also apply to a verse with the same meaning, which the protesters sometimes use: "If children, then heirs—heirs of God and joint heirs with Christ, if indeed we suffer with Him, that we may also be glorified together."[480]

The Fifth Protest

"The one who comes to Me I will by no means cast out"
(John 6:37).

It is true that the one who comes to Christ, He will by no means cast out. What do we say, however, about the ones who cast themselves out of their own accord, by their own will? Christ is the door; If anyone enters by Him, he will be saved and will go in and out and find pasture.[481] All those who left the holy sheepfold left by themselves, their works, their recklessness, their error. They willed for themselves perdition. On such as these, St. John the Apostle says, "They went out from us, but they were not of us; for if they had been of us, they would have continued with us."[482] They were the ones who went out.

Of these were those who did not endure the words of the Lord Christ when He spoke about partaking of His body and blood. On this, the Scripture says, "From that time many of His disciples went back and walked with Him no more. Then Jesus said to the twelve, 'Do you also want to go away?'"[483] These the Lord did not

---

478 Matthew 7:21.
479 Matthew 12:50.
480 Romans 8:17.
481 See John 10:9.
482 1 John 2:19.
483 John 6:66–67.

cast out, but they themselves were the ones who left him, contrary to the twelve who continued steadfastly with Him. Even Judas Iscariot also the Lord did not cast out; rather, he abandoned the community of the disciples and abandoned the Lord's Supper and left to do what he had previously conspired to do.

The Sixth Protest

"He who has the Son has life."
(1 John 5:11–12)

Some protest with the saying of St. John the Apostle: "And this is the testimony: that God has given us eternal life, and this life is in His Son. He who has the Son has life; he who does not have the Son of God does not have life."[484] They say, "So long as a person has life and has eternal life, how then does the person perish?"

The key to this verse is understanding the intended meaning of the phrase "he who has the Son." So, what does this phrase mean? Does it mean "he who believes in Him"? No, of course not, because the Son Himself says, "Not everyone who says to Me, 'Lord, Lord,' shall enter the kingdom of heaven, but he who does the will of My Father in heaven."[485] The Lord continued His word, saying, "Many will say to Me in that day, 'Lord, Lord, have we not prophesied in Your name, cast out demons in Your name, and done many wonders in Your name?' And then I will declare to them, 'I never knew you; depart from Me, you who practice lawlessness!'"[486] Not only were these believers, but also performers of miracles. Nevertheless, they did not have the Son: "He never knew them."[487] This is because they practiced lawlessness.

Likewise were the foolish virgins: they were believers, and they

---

484   1 John 5:11–12.
485   Matthew 7:21.
486   Matthew 7:22–23.
487   Cf. Matthew 7:23.

called Him, saying, "Lord, Lord, open to us!"[488] But He answered them, saying, "Assuredly, I say to you, I do not know you."[489] Then the phrase "he who has the Son" does not mean just faith [in Him]. What does it mean then? What is the meaning of "He who has the Son has life"? It means the following.

1. *Knowing the Son:*

This is clear from the saying of our Lord Jesus Christ Himself to the Father, "This is eternal life, that they may know You, the only true God, and Jesus Christ whom You have sent."[490] What, however, is the meaning that we know the Son? And what is the proof that we have known Him? St. John the Apostle himself answers in the same epistle, saying:

> Now by this we know that we know Him, if we keep His commandments. He who says, "I know Him," and does not keep His commandments, is a liar, and the truth is not in him. But whoever keeps His word, truly the love of God is perfected in him. By this we know that we are in Him.[491]

This is the response, because how do we have the Son if we do not know Him? Or, how do we know Him if we do not keep His commandments? So if we keep His commandments, by this we indicate that we know Him; and if we know Him, we have life. Then the one who keeps the commandments of the Son, has the Son, and has life. And keeping the commandments is nothing but works that prove the truth of this keeping [of the commandments].

2. *Abiding in the Son*

The one who has the Son is he who abides in the Son. And the Son Himself said, "Abide in Me, and I in you…. I am the vine, you are the branches…. If anyone does not abide in Me, he is cast out as a branch and is withered; and they gather them and throw them into

---

488 Matthew 25:11.
489 Matthew 25:12.
490 John 17:3.
491 1 John 2:3–5.

the fire, and they are burned."[492] So abiding in Him is necessary for life, as a branch does not live unless it abides in the vine. And the one who does not abide in it withers, and its end is the fire. Then the one who abides in the Son has life.

So, how do we abide in Him? The Son continues His word, saying, "Abide in My love. If you keep My commandments, you will abide in My love, just as I have kept My Father's commandments and abide in His love."[493] The matter then, in this respect also, is related to keeping the commandments, that is, to do good works. St. John the beloved confirms this also in his same epistle, saying, "He who says he abides in Him ought himself also to walk just as He walked."[494] What else does the phrase "He who has the Son" mean?

3. Fellowship with the Son

The one who has the Son is the one who has fellowship with Him. On this, St. John the Apostle himself says, "And truly our fellowship is with the Father and with His Son Jesus Christ."[495] St. Paul the Apostle speaks copiously about this fellowship, saying, "We died with Him; we were buried with Him; we were raised with Him; we are glorified with Him."[496] He also says, "That I may know Him and the power of His resurrection, and the fellowship of His sufferings,"[497] and says, "I have been crucified with Christ,"[498] and so on. But how do we have fellowship with Him? Here, St. John answers in the same epistle, "If we say that we have fellowship with Him, and walk in darkness, we lie and do not practice the truth. But if we walk in the light as He is in the light, we have fellowship with one another, and the blood of Jesus Christ His Son cleanses us from all sin."[499] The matter then is as before, related to conduct, that is, to works.

---

492 John 15:4–6.
493 John 15:9–10.
494 1 John 2:6.
495 1 John 1:3.
496 See Romans 6.
497 Philippians 3:10.
498 Galatians 2:2.
499 1 John 1:6–7.

4. *Loving the Son*

There is no doubt that the one who has the Son is connected to the Son through the bond of love. So, how do we love Him then? The Lord Christ Himself answers this question by saying, "He who has My commandments and keeps them, it is he who loves Me. And he who loves Me will be loved by My Father, and I will love him and manifest Myself to him."[500] St. John confirms this also in the same epistle, saying, "For this is the love of God, that we keep His commandments."[501] The matter from this aspect is also related to keeping the commandments, that is, to works.

Therefore, the phrase "He who has the Son"—whether it meant "he who knows the Son," or "he who abides in the Son," or "he who has fellowship with the Son," or "he who loves the Son"— requires the keeping of the commandments, so that the believer may have eternal life. Thus, eternal life requires a continuous walking in righteousness. If a person deviates from it, they lose this life, because "if we say that we have fellowship with Him, and walk in darkness, we lie and do not practice the truth."[502] St. John's first epistle has a particular spirit permeating through the whole epistle. Therefore, if the Protestants tried to depend on a single verse from it, they would find the response to them in the rest of the epistle.

⸺

The Seventh Protest

The Example of the Passover Lamb
(Exodus 12:23, 7)

"When He sees the blood on the lintel and on the two doorposts, the Lord will pass over the door and not allow the destroyer to come into your houses to strike you."[503] The protesters exploit this verse and say: "Those who sought refuge within the doors smeared

---

500 John 14:21.
501 1 John 5:3.
502 1 John 1:6.
503 Exodus 12:23.

with blood, felt perfectly safe and reassured regardless of their personal state, and regardless of their shortcomings and iniquities, because their salvation depended on the blood, the blood of the Passover lamb which is a symbol for Christ. And their salvation did not at all depend on their works." And they say that we must have the fullness of confidence in the blood of Christ, looking to the merits of the blood and not to our works.

We do not deny that salvation was accomplished by the blood of Christ alone, and that the propitiation of the blood of Christ is infinite, sufficient to send reassurance into the soul. Our confidence in the blood of Christ, however, does not mean that we live in sin or that we neglect any good work, claiming that our salvation depends on the blood and not on our righteousness and purity.

In the example of the Passover lamb and the doors sprinkled with blood, we see a very important note that explains the situation in a sound manner with respect to the symbol: the Passover lamb was eaten with unleavened bread,[504] and all leaven was removed from the camp for seven days. And so does the Scripture say, "Seven days you shall eat unleavened bread, and on the seventh day there shall be a feast to the LORD. Unleavened bread shall be eaten seven days. And no leavened bread shall be seen among you, nor shall leaven be seen among you in all your quarters."[505]

The Lord greatly emphasized the removal of leaven from the houses, and whoever ate leavened bread was to be cut off as a punishment. The Scripture said, "Seven days you shall eat unleavened bread. On the first day you shall remove leaven from your houses. For whoever eats leavened bread from the first day until the seventh day, that person shall be cut off from Israel."[506] And He reiterated and emphasized this point again, saying, "You shall eat unleavened bread.... For seven days no leaven shall be found in your houses, since whoever eats what is leavened, that same person shall be cut off from the congregation of Israel, whether he is a stranger or a native of the land. You shall eat nothing leavened;

---

504 See Exodus 12:8.
505 Exodus 13:6–7.
506 Exodus 12:15.

in all your dwellings you shall eat unleavened bread."[507]

So what is the wisdom in all this? What is it a symbol of? Anyone who studies the Holy Scriptures would clearly see that leaven is a symbol of evil and sin, and that the unleavened bread is a symbol of righteousness and purity. St. Paul the Apostle made this matter perfectly clear when he said:

> Therefore purge out the old leaven, that you may be a new lump, since you truly are unleavened. For indeed Christ, our Passover, was sacrificed for us. Therefore let us keep the feast, not with old leaven, nor with the leaven of malice and wickedness, but with the unleavened bread of sincerity and truth.[508]

Thus, the picture is made clear before us: from outside the door is sprinkled with blood, and from inside the leaven is removed, and all eat unleavened bread. The blood of Christ cannot be a permit for us to eat leaven. And the soul of the person, who escapes the sword of the destroyer through the blood, may be cut off from the congregation if he eats leavened bread despite this first salvation. And so he loses the salvation of the blood through eating leavened bread. How many people were saved from the Original Sin by the blood of Christ and were delivered from the sword of the destroyer, and then lost this salvation and were cut off from the body of the Church, because they ate leavened bread, those "whose end is destruction, whose god is their belly, and whose glory is in their shame—who set their mind on earthly things."[509]

Do you, after this, dare to say, "I sleep reassured within the doors sprinkled with blood, regardless of my conduct"? I say to you, "No, if leaven is found within your doors, you cannot sleep reassured. 'Since whoever eats what is leavened, that same person shall be cut off from the congregation.'[510]" Therefore purge out the old leaven and keep the feast with the unleavened bread of sincerity

---

507 Exodus 12:18–20.
508 1 Corinthians 5:7–8.
509 Philippians 3:19.
510 Exodus 12:19.

and truth. The seven days of unleavened bread symbolize the whole life, which must be pure, because seven is a number that represents perfection. And so long, brother, as you are living within the doors sprinkled with blood, be careful throughout your life that you remove the leaven from your house, because the judgment is clear.

The Eighth Protest

Christ Satisfied the Requirements of God

The protesters say, "The death of Christ has satisfied the requirements of divine justice from all sides. So does God require us to satisfy them again?" No, God does not require us to do that. Also, we are weaker than to be able to fulfill the justice of God. The Lord Christ has truly satisfied all the requirements of divine justice, and He offered an infinite propitiation, sufficient to remit all sins of all people in all generations. But we reiterate here what we have already said, that the blood of Christ is one thing and being worthy of the blood of Christ is another thing. All that we do is not that we satisfy the requirements of divine justice, but rather that we may be found worthy of the merits we receive by the blood of Christ. We do not try to fulfill the due of divine justice; this was accomplished on the cross, when the Lord shed His blood for us. Rather, all that we do is to be worthy of the blood of Christ.

The Ninth Protest

"He who hears My word ... has everlasting life"

They also protest by the saying of the Lord, "He who hears My word and believes in Him who sent Me has everlasting life, and shall not come into judgment, but has passed from death into life."[511] We note here that He is not speaking about faith only, but also about works even more, in saying "he who hears My word," that is, "he who carries out My commandments." And we believe that the believer who carries out God's commandments to the end—this is the one who is saved. And if we followed the rest of the Lord's speech on this occasion, we would find Him say, "… and [all will] come forth—those who have done good, to the resurrection of life,"[512] and He did not say "those who have believed," emphasizing the important of works for salvation.

The Tenth Protest

"He who promised is faithful"
(Hebrews 10:23).

It is true that the promise of God is present, and He who promised is faithful, but this does not invite us to blind confidence. St. Paul himself, however, warns us in the same epistle, saying, "Therefore, since a promise remains of entering His rest, let us fear lest any of you seem to have come short of it,"[513] and he says, "If we deny Him, He also will deny us."[514] My brethren, always remember the danger of using "the single verse."

When do we Attain Salvation?

If it were possible for the believer to fall and to perish, and if there were people who began in the Spirit and [yet] finished in the flesh, when would we then say about a person that they are fully saved? We say this when the person completes the days of their pilgrimage on the earth in peace. This is because we are in a

---

511 John 5:24.
512 John 5:29.
513 Hebrews 4:1.
514 2 Timothy 2:12.

war and conflict. So long as we are in the body,[515] we are in a war whose outcome we do not know yet, because it is possible for a person to win the first round but lose in the twelfth round. Who can guarantee? A warrior cannot say that he won except after the end of the war, that is, after putting off this body. Therefore, the Apostle says, "Work out your own salvation with fear and trembling,"[516] and also says, "Considering the outcome of their conduct."[517]

Holy Scriptures About Our Awaited Salvation

✣ St. Paul says, "For our citizenship is in heaven, from which we also eagerly wait for the Savior, the Lord Jesus Christ, who will transform our lowly body that it may be conformed to His glorious body."[518] This is salvation when we put off this mortal body and put on the glorious body, after the second coming of Christ and the general resurrection.

✣ He also says, "So Christ was offered once to bear the sins of many. To those who eagerly wait for Him He will appear a second time, apart from sin, for salvation."[519] The Apostle here also speaks about the final salvation, which will happen after Christ's second coming.

✣ Likewise, St. Peter the Apostle says, "[You] who are kept by the power of God through faith for salvation ready to be revealed in the last time."[520]

✣ St. Paul explained this same truth when he commanded concerning the sinner of Corinth: "Deliver such a one to Satan for the destruction of the flesh, that his spirit may be saved in the day of the Lord Jesus."[521]

---

515 See Ephesians 6:12.
516 Philippians 2:12.
517 Hebrews 13:7.
518 Philippians 3:20–21.
519 Hebrews 9:28.
520 1 Peter 1:5.
521 1 Corinthians 5:5.

✤ Concerning this coming salvation, the Apostle says to the Romans, "For now our salvation is nearer than when we first believed."[522]

✤ And he says to his disciple Timothy the Bishop, "Take heed to yourself and to the doctrine. Continue in them, for in doing this you will save both yourself and those who hear you."[523] So this saint was in need of taking heed to himself and taking heed to the doctrine, and of continuing to take heed, so that he may be saved.

✤ Concerning this awaited salvation, St. Peter the Apostle says, "If the righteous one is scarcely saved…"[524]

✤ St. Paul says about the angels, "Are they not all ministering spirits sent forth to minister for those who will inherit salvation?"[525]

✤ This final salvation requires endurance and struggle, so that we may attain it in glory. On this, St. Paul says, "Therefore I endure all things for the sake of the elect, that they also may obtain the salvation which is in Christ Jesus with eternal glory."[526] Then those elect did not receive the salvation in which is eternal glory, although they received salvation by the blood of Christ in Baptism. It is, however, merely a pledge[527] which we could lose if we cease to struggle, and our will be deviated.

✤ This final salvation—how do we attain it? The Apostle answers, saying, "Let us run with endurance the race that is set before us."[528] "He who endures to the end shall be saved."[529]

---

522 Romans 13:11.
523 1 Timothy 4:16.
524 1 Peter 4:18.
525 Hebrews 1:14.
526 2 Timothy 2:10.
527 See Ephesians 1:14.
528 Hebrews 12:1.
529 Matthew 24:13.

CHAPTER SIX

The Answers to Questions Related to the Subject

Has God Chosen People Predestined for Salvation?

1. Salvation is Offered to All

The Scripture gives a clear answer to this question, saying, "For this is good and acceptable in the sight of God our Savior, who desires all men to be saved and to come to the knowledge of the truth."[530] God desires all people to be saved, and not [only] a particular group of them. The love of God has encompassed the whole world; therefore, He says, "I have no pleasure in the death of the wicked, but that the wicked turn from his way and live."[531]

For this reason, on the issue of redemption, the Scripture says, "For God so loved the world that He gave His only begotten Son, that whoever believes in Him should not perish but have everlasting life."[532] Here we see that His love is for all in general, for the whole world; and salvation is offered in general to whoever believes in Him [as] a redeemer, and not to a specific group. This same understanding is also repeated by St. John the Beloved, when speaking on the propitiative sacrifice of Christ, saying, "And He Himself is the propitiation for our sins, and not for ours only but

---

530 1 Timothy 2:3–4.
531 Ezekiel 33:11.
532 John 3:16.

also for the whole world."[533] The Lord Christ, then, has offered salvation to all, giving Himself for all. He is the propitiation for the sins of the whole world, desiring all to be saved.

Our teacher Peter the Apostle explains this generality, saying, "In truth I perceive that God shows no partiality. But in every nation whoever fears Him and works righteousness is accepted by Him.... He is Lord of all."[534] This also resembles what St. Peter said on the Day of Pentecost: "And it shall come to pass that whoever calls on the name of the LORD shall be saved."[535] Then God desires all people to be saved; if all are not saved, the reason cannot be ascribed to God, but rather to people, because they themselves did not desire salvation for their souls, and it is not God who did not desire salvation for them.

2. God Put the Choice in People's Hands

God, as a good and lover [of mankind], does not desire the death of a single sinner, but desires that every sinner may return and live; nevertheless, He has put the choice in people's hands, leaving the liberty to every person to choose for themselves. On this, the Master Lord says to the person:

> See, I have set before you today life and good, death and evil.... I call heaven and earth as witnesses today against you, that I have set before you life and death, blessing and cursing; therefore choose life, that both you and your descendants may live.[536]

If the choice was not in a person's hand, why then did God send the apostles and prophets? Why then did He give us the commandments and offer the warnings? Why did He appoint priests and teachers? What is the benefit of all this if there are people predestined for salvation, and others predestined for perdition?

---

533 1 John 2:2.
534 Acts 10:34–36.
535 Acts 2:21.
536 Deuteronomy 30:15, 19.

3. Many Scriptures Indicate That the Will is in the Person's Hand

Many of the holy commandments of God begin with the phrase "if anyone desires," "if you want," or "if anyone hears," and similar such phrases, which indicate that the will is in a person's hand. They choose for themselves whatever they desire, determining their fate according to their work. We will give examples of all these.

Our Lord Jesus Christ said, "If anyone desires to come after Me, let him deny himself, and take up his cross, and follow Me. For whoever desires to save his life will lose it, but whoever loses his life for My sake will find it."[537] And He said to the rich young man, "But if you want to enter into life, keep the commandments…. If you want to be perfect, go, sell what you have and give to the poor."[538] And He said in His letter to the angel of the church in Laodicea, "Behold, I stand at the door and knock. If anyone hears My voice and opens the door, I will come in to him and dine with him, and he with Me."[539] With respect to God, He is standing, knocking at the door; and with respect to a person, they possess the choice: to open or not to open. And as a result of this, their fate is determined.

Many a time God desires, and [yet] the person does not desire. God desires good for a person, and [yet] the person does not desire good for himself. And God leaves the person to their free will, to meet their fate according to what he desires. An example of this is the saying of the Lord in His lamentation over Jerusalem, "How often I wanted to gather your children together, as a hen gathers her chicks under her wings, but you were not willing! See! Your house is left to you desolate."[540] And another example of this also is the Lord's rebuke for the Jews when He said to them, "You are not willing to come to Me that you may have life."[541]

---

537 Matthew 16:24–25.
538 Matthew 19:17, 21.
539 Revelation 3:20.
540 Matthew 23:37–38.
541 John 5:40.

On this subject is also included the parable of the wedding feast and those invited. The Lord said about the master of the wedding feast, "[He] sent out his servants to call those who were invited to the wedding; and they were not willing to come."[542] They are invited to the wedding and are not prepared for perdition [by the master of the wedding]. God opens the kingdom to them, but they refuse to go in. In this parable of the wedding feast, we find that the invitation was repeated more than once and twice. Every time the master sends other servants to those invited, but they do not desire to come. Therefore, this tragedy was ended by the master saying to his servants, "The wedding is ready, but those who were invited were not worthy."[543]

One of the most profound examples of the extent of God's care about the will of a person in determining one's fate is that the Lord Christ—glory be to Him—says to the man who was sick, before healing him, "Do you want to be made well?"[544] The great Physician is ready to heal, but the problem of those who perish is that they do not want to be made well.

4. God is Ready to Turn from His Judgment

Is there a clearer proof than this, of the depth of God's desire to care for our salvation? If a person turns from their evil and seeks salvation for themselves, there is no objection with God to turn from His judgment. God declares this truth, saying:

> Again, when I say to the wicked, "You shall surely die," if he turns from his sin and does what is lawful and right … and walks in the statutes of life without committing iniquity, he shall surely live; he shall not die. None of his sins which he has committed shall be remembered against him; he has done what is lawful and right; he shall surely live.[545]

---

542 Matthew 22:3.
543 Matthew 22:8.
544 John 5:6.
545 Ezekiel 33:14–16.

This same meaning, God also mentioned in the Book of Jeremiah the prophet, saying:

> The instant I speak concerning a nation and concerning a kingdom, to pluck up, to pull down, and to destroy it, if that nation against whom I have spoken turns from its evil, I will relent of the disaster that I thought to bring upon it. And the instant I speak concerning a nation and concerning a kingdom, to build and to plant it, if it does evil in My sight so that it does not obey My voice, then I will relent concerning the good with which I said I would benefit it.[546]

We have a clear, practical example in the story of Nineveh: God decreed a judgment against it, but the people of Nineveh repented through the preaching of Jonah. And so the Scripture says, "Then God saw their works, that they turned from their evil way; and God relented from the disaster that He had said He would bring upon them, and He did not do it."[547] The matter, then, depends on the person. Therefore, our teacher James the Apostle says, "Draw near to God and He will draw near to you."[548] God Himself says in the Book of Malachi the prophet, "Return to Me, and I will return to you."[549]

5. Responding to Some Protests

First, we begin with the saying of St. Paul the Apostle in his epistle to the Romans, "And we know that all things work together for good to those who love God, to those who are the called according to His purpose. For whom He foreknew, He also predestined to be conformed to the image of His Son..."[550] In this Scripture, we observe the following important, fundamental notes: he said, "all things work together for good to those who love God" and not

---

546 Jeremiah 18:7–10.
547 Jonah 3:10.
548 James 4:8.
549 Malachi 3:7.
550 Romans 8:28–30.

"those whom God loves," for the matter depends on them, not on Him. This also applies to the saying of St. Paul the Apostle, "But as it is written: 'Eye has not seen, nor ear heard, nor have entered into the heart of man the things which God has prepared for those who love Him.'"[551] Neither did he say "those whom God loves," for the matter concerning their salvation depends on their own will.

The second note is that the predestination of God does not refer to being chosen by God, but to His foreknowledge: as he said, "For whom He foreknew, He also predestined." God, through His foreknowledge and His awareness of what will happen in the future time, knew those who would walk according to His pleasure, in righteousness and uprightness by their full choice. And those whom He foreknew, He also predestined.

This word also applies to the story of Jacob and Esau: "Jacob I have loved, but Esau I have hated."[552] For God, through His foreknowledge, knew that Esau would be profane and a murderer, who would despise the birthright, selling it for one morsel of lentil; He also knew the meekness of Jacob and his love for goodness. So God loved in Jacob what He saw in him through His foreknowledge, and hated in Esau what He saw he would do through His foreknowledge also. But we cannot at all say that God predestined Esau for perdition, and predestined Jacob for salvation, meaning that He wrote on Esau perdition regardless of his choice, and that He chose Jacob for salvation regardless of his works! God forbid that He would do this.

After this comes the saying of the Scripture, "Will the thing formed say to him who formed it, 'Why have you made me like this?' Does not the potter have power over the clay, from the same lump to make one vessel for honor and another for dishonor?"[553] Yes, the potter has power over the clay, to make from it what he desires, a vessel for honor or for dishonor, and the clay does not have [power] to say to him, "Why have you made me like this?" The potter, however, is also wise and just.

---

551 1 Corinthians 2:9.

552 Romans 9:13.

553 Romans 9:20–21.

One of the beautiful explanations I heard on this subject is that the potter, with his full freedom and power, looks with wisdom at the lump of clay and examines it. If he saw that it was good, smooth, soft, and fit to be a vessel for honor, then he would of necessity make it a vessel for honor. It is unreasonable that a wonderful [lump of] clay falls into the hand of the potter, and he makes from it a vessel for dishonor, because the potter is wise. If the [lump of] clay were rough, bad, and unfit to be a vessel for honor, then the potter would be obliged, according to what suits its condition, to make from it a vessel for dishonor.

The matter before all else, then, depends on the state of the clay and the extent of its suitability, although we admit the power and freedom of the potter. The potter, as much as he can, tries to make from the clay that is in front of him a vessel for honor, as much as the clay assists him in doing so. Therefore, the Lord said:

> Look, as the clay is in the potter's hand, so are you in My hand, O house of Israel! The instant I speak concerning a nation and concerning a kingdom, to pluck up, to pull down, and to destroy it, if that nation against whom I have spoken turns from its evil, I will relent of the disaster that I thought to bring upon it. And the instant I speak concerning a nation and concerning a kingdom, to build and to plant it, if it does evil in My sight so that it does not obey My voice, then I will relent concerning the good with which I said I would benefit it.[554]

This reminds us of the parable of the sower who went out to sow:[555] the sower is the same sower, and the seed is the same seed, but according to the nature of the earth onto which the seed fell, so was its end result, either damaging [the seed] or bringing forth fruit [from the seed]. The sower did not prepare some seed for them to be withered away, or to be scorched, or to be choked, or to be eaten by birds. The nature of the earth, however, was in control of the matter. The person is free, then, to choose his fate: "For he who

---

554 Jeremiah 18:6–10.
555 Matthew 13:3–8.

sows to his flesh will of the flesh reap corruption, but he who sows to the Spirit will of the Spirit reap everlasting life."[556]

6. Studying the Matter from the Theological Aspect

In this principle of choosing, there is injustice and partiality, and it does not agree with the justice of God, who "will render to each one according to his deeds."[557] If God had mercy on whomever He had mercy, and had compassion on whomever He had compassion, and left the rest to perdition, how would this be in agreement with God's justice? Those whom God predestined for perdition, what is their guilt? Does not this lead sinners to fall into despair, feeling that there is no benefit to their struggle, so long as they are vessels prepared for dishonor? As for the righteous, this undoubtedly drives them to slothfulness and negligence, feeling that they are saved no matter what, whether they struggle or not.

Then, what is the meaning of recompense if there are people on whom perdition is written before they are born, while for others salvation is written before they are born? What is, then, the merit of the elect so that they are rewarded? What is the guilt of the evildoers so that they are punished? What is the need for the commandment, then, if the fate of a person is inevitable, whether they obey the commandment or not? Then, is this principle of choosing not in disagreement with man's free will?

What is the devil's benefit in testing a person's will? What is the use of his labor in tempting the elect, while they are inevitably saved, regardless of his temptations? What is the use of his labor in making those who are not chosen fall, while they are perishing, even if he does not fight against them?

What is the necessity of evangelism, preaching, guiding, and teaching, if these will change nothing of what was written for the person, of either being chosen or rejected?

This idea of choosing makes the world fall into confusion,

---

556 Galatians 6:8.
557 Romans 2:6.

and it is inconsistent with the justice of God, and it is also in disagreement with man's free will.

What was the Struggle of the Thief so That He was Saved?

Those who claim that salvation is by faith alone ask: "What good works did the right-hand thief do and what was his struggle, so that he was saved?" We answer that the thief did many things, most important of which are the following.

1. The Thief Believed in the Lord Under Very Difficult Circumstances

The mere believing was not an easy matter for the thief. Had he believed in the Lord while He raised the dead, healed the sick, walked on water, rebuked the wind, and performed supernatural miracles, we would have said that the matters were clear and accepted without doubt. He believed in Christ, however, while He was crucified; he believed in Him while He was shamefully treated and held in contempt by people, and before all, He was in a state of weakness; they slapped Him, spit in His face, mocked Him, saying to Him, "Prophesy! Who is the one who struck You?"[558]

Many resisting forces were on every side against this faith. If this thief had not believed, people would have made excuses for him, saying, "How can he believe in a crucified man, shamefully treated, that He is God?" The thief must have needed great struggle with himself internally to [reach] this faith, fighting the many doubts that stood before him and that were about to terminate his faith.

Everyone who says that the thief did not struggle seems to have not imagined nor pictured the situation that surrounded the thief, that situation which made most people stumble, even the disciples to whom the Lord said, "All of you will be made to stumble because

---

558 Luke 22:64.

of Me this night, for it is written: 'I will strike the Shepherd, and the sheep will be scattered.'"[559] And indeed all the followers were scattered, and no one was able to stand beside the cross except only the women named Mary and John the beloved—and this thief!

The veil of the temple was torn in two, the sun was darkened, and the rocks were split; so, were these sufficient for him to believe? We know well that, despite all these, the high priests, the priests, the elders, the scribes, and the Pharisees did not believe. Also, the other thief did not believe. The faith of the right-hand thief was not a simple matter.

2. He Confessed the Lord with Perfect Confession

The phrase, "Lord, remember me when You come into Your kingdom,"[560] carries many meanings: he had confessed the crucified Christ [as] a Lord, and confessed Him also [as] a king. He confessed that Christ has a kingdom, and that He is coming into His kingdom, that is, that death has no power over Him. He also believed that Christ is able to bring him into the kingdom; that is, he believed that his salvation would be at the hand of this [Man] who was crucified with him.

This thief had a great hope. Despite all the appalling evils he had done in his life, he believed that a person like him could be saved and enter the kingdom through Christ.

This thief was not content with his faith; rather, he confessed this faith publicly, before all, without shame, a matter which St. Peter the Apostle and most of the disciples and apostles were not able to do. Not only did the thief confess his faith in Christ, but he also confessed his sins.

3. He Also Confessed His Sins

The thief was not content with confessing his faith, but holy zeal took hold of him when he heard his companion blaspheming

---

559 Mark 14:27.
560 Luke 23:42.

Christ, saying, "If You are the Christ, save Yourself and us."[561] The right-hand thief answered him, rebukingly, "Do you not even fear God, seeing you are under the same condemnation? And we indeed justly, for we receive the due reward of our deeds; but this Man has done nothing wrong."[562] And so the thief confessed his sins and confessed that he was worthy of punishment. He confessed that, by dying crucified, he received the due recompense of his deeds. It was as though he did not regard that the sentence was great enough, but rather he said, "We indeed [were punished] justly."

This thief was spiritual in his approach: for while the other thief was thinking of a way to be rescued from death and crucifixion, saying, "Save Yourself and us,"[563] this believing thief was thinking about his eternity and about the kingdom. And he entreated the Lord for the sake of his eternal salvation, not for the sake of rescuing him from the death of the body. With respect to the death of the body, the right-hand thief was content with it as a punishment for his sins; he, however, found these moments necessary for him to think about his eternity. And his mind was preoccupied with the Lord and His kingdom. Therefore, we see him defending the Lord.

4. He Defended the Lord

Christ stood alone, and no one defended Him, of those who enjoyed His gifts and miracles. No one defended Him, of His Apostles, nor of those who followed Him, with the exception of a few names. The voice of this thief was raised, putting to shame thousands of those who were ungrateful, by saying, "But this Man has done nothing wrong."[564] A marvelous defense from a person welcoming death, with which he proved that humanity still had a remnant of good. Therefore, he was worthy that the Lord say to him, "Today you will be with Me in Paradise."[565]

---

561 Luke 23:39.
562 Luke 23:40–41.
563 Luke 23:39.
564 Luke 23:41.
565 Luke 23:43.

Should people then ask and say, "What was the struggle of the thief, and what did he do?" I ask all of them another question, which I would be pleased to hear an answer to: "What was this thief able to do more than these, and did not do it?"

How Were They Saved Without Baptism?

Some ask: "How were the martyrs saved without Baptism? And how was this right-hand thief saved without Baptism too, so long as Baptism is necessary for salvation?"

We have previously explained that Baptism, in its essence, is death with Christ; therefore, St. Paul the Apostle said, "Do you not know that as many of us as were baptized into Christ Jesus were baptized into His death? Therefore we were buried with Him through baptism into death.... Now if we died with Christ, we believe that we shall also live with Him."[566] Likewise, the martyrs died with Christ; they participated with Him in death and in the shedding of their blood. Therefore, the Church calls such a death the baptism of blood. And if these had been given an opportunity to live longer, they would have fulfilled the Baptism of water also.

---

566 Romans 6:3–4, 8. See also Romans 6:3–8.

www.ingramcontent.com/pod-product-compliance
Lightning Source LLC
LaVergne TN
LVHW090046090426

835511LV00031B/322